Praise for *Role Call*

Role Call is filled with effective instructional strategies to truly transform your teaching practice. Whether you are a new or seasoned teacher, you will benefit from Dr. Copper's thoughtful instructional planning, engaging lessons, and practical implementation. The new perspectives and lenses provided in this book will help teachers ignite their instruction with inspiration, passion, and creativity. As a high school English teacher, I am excited to add new lenses to my teaching toolkit.

—**Christina Schneider,** author of *Building Strong Writers*

Trying a new lens can open a whole new world of possibilities and perspectives! Full of immersive exercises and useful examples, *Role Call* gives educators the lenses they need to plan engaging lessons from different angles. Whether you reach for an archetype lens, an artistic lens, or an array of other lenses, your next lesson plan just got a lot more interesting!

—**Ashley Bible,** coauthor of *Keeping the Wonder*

Role Call by Dr. Jenna Copper is a fantastic book for young professionals and those entering the field of education. It serves as a tool for reflection and self-discovery. This engaging book allows readers to connect with the material and learn more about themselves. My favorite parts are the interactive sections, where readers can journal their responses. This book encourages readers to be their authentic selves.

—**Dr. Samantha Fecich,** author of *EduMagic: A Guide for Preservice Teachers* and host of the *EduMagic* podcast

Jenna offers an all-in-one-resource with interactive questions, engaging visual aids, insightful teacher testimonies, and practical lesson templates to empower educators. She invites us to authentically step into our roles, inspiring us to cultivate the same leadership within our students. With her guidance, we are not simply exploring different perspectives; we're invited to embark on the transformative journey together.

—**Staci Lamb,** coauthor of *Keeping the Wonder* and Cecil County Teacher of the Year

ROLE CALL

ROLE CALL

PLAN with Perspective,
CREATE High-Engagement Lessons, and
UNLEASH Your Creative Teaching Potential

JENNA COPPER, PHD

Role Call: Plan with Perspective, Create High-Engagement Lessons, and Unleash Your Creative Teaching Potential
© 2024 Jenna Copper

All rights reserved. No part of this publication may be reproduced in any form or by any electronic or mechanical means, including information storage and retrieval systems, without permission in writing by the publisher, except by a reviewer who may quote brief passages in a review. For information regarding permission, contact the publisher at books@daveburgessconsulting.com.

> This book is available at special discounts when purchased in quantity for educational purposes or for use as premiums, promotions, or fundraisers. For inquiries and details, contact the publisher at books@daveburgessconsulting.com.

Published by Dave Burgess Consulting, Inc.
Vancouver, WA
DaveBurgessConsulting.com

Library of Congress Control Number: 2024947493
Paperback ISBN: 978-1-956306-89-7
Ebook ISBN: 978-1-956306-90-3

Cover and interior design by Liz Schreiter
Edited and produced by Reading List Editorial
ReadingListEditorial.com

For Mike

CONTENTS

Introduction 1

PART 1: YOUR ROLE

Chapter 1: Who Are You? 6
Chapter 2: Who Do You Want to Be? 27
Chapter 3: What Is Your Role? 41

PART 2: YOUR STUDENTS' ROLES

Chapter 4: Find Your New Perspective(s) 64
Chapter 5: Give Them a Role 82
Chapter 6: Create Your Own Vision 93
Conclusion: Admire the View 109

About the Author 125
Acknowledgments 127
Endnotes 128
More from Dave Burgess Consulting, Inc. 135

INTRODUCTION

Let's begin with a question. If someone asked, "Who are you?" what would you say?

You'd probably start with your name. "Hi, I'm [insert your name]," you'd reply.

But what if that person probed a little more deeply: "No, I mean *really* who are you?"

"Ah, so they're getting existential. Well, I can match that," you'd think to yourself. "I'm a mom and a sister, a yogi and a reader, a chef and a chauffeur, a history buff and alliteration lover, a poet and a shutterbug, and, of course, a teacher." *Ta-da!*

Poetic, isn't it?

We all have different roles in this life: those we cherish, those we take on begrudgingly, and those we do without even thinking. These roles make up who we are. You're reading this book, so it's a safe bet that the role of teacher is a big part of your identity.

Being a teacher is so much more than a job. It's a role only other teachers can truly understand and appreciate. It means a sleepless night before the first day of school (in year one and year twenty) and a keen sense of the approaching full moon. It means you deliver a lesson that flops in the same week you teach the best lesson of your life. It means forgetting to take attendance and rushing to the copier to pick up your worksheet right before class.

It means embracing a role. A role that is equally challenging and rewarding.

I've always been interested in roles. In second grade, I made my acting debut (and finale) as La Befana in the school play. In sixth grade, I wrote a play called *Sleeping Ugly*, a retelling of the classic *Sleeping Beauty* story. In ninth grade, I dressed up as Janet Reno for a speech in history class. In twelfth grade, as the oldest child in my family, I researched the effect of my birth order on my personality. In college, I assumed the role of an English major. As a young adult, I became a teacher.

Then, in grad school, I turned my fascination with roles into research. My 2013 dissertation study explored how to bring multiple perspectives, or "literary lenses," as I like to call them, to English language arts (ELA) classes.[1] I tweaked and refined this concept during my time as a secondary ELA teacher until I accepted a new position in 2022: professor in an education department, working with preservice teachers and their K–12 cooperating teachers. This perspective has been one of the most fascinating of all. I now get to tap into the roles of hundreds (if not thousands) of teachers and students from grades K–12.

In spring 2023, I was observing Tyler Dickson, a student teacher in a third-grade classroom. Before beginning his read-aloud for the day, he asked, "Why is it valuable to learn about other people's cultures?"

A small hand shot into the air before he could even finish the question. I smiled at her eagerness.

She responded by saying, "We're all a little different, but really, we're all the same." She continued, "We all have a lot in common, but we can learn a lot from what makes us different."

The wisdom of that nine-year-old is something I've been thinking about for a while now. We do have a lot in common. We share so many roles. Still, we can learn so much from what makes us different, the roles that make us unique.

That young student summarized in thirty seconds what I've been studying for more than a decade: the power of perspective in teaching and learning.

I've written this book because I'm ready to answer the role call.

Since you picked up this book, I know you are, too.

The Path Ahead

In this book, I'm going to teach you what I've learned about the power of perspective in teaching and learning. These lessons come out of a decade-long exploration that continues today. *Role Call* is a call to action. It means being present to discover your authentic teaching role so you can lead students down a meaningful path of learning. Therefore, this book is divided into two parts: your role and your students' role.

Part 1 is dedicated to you. Refining, discovering, understanding, and celebrating your role as a teacher is the first step in this system. Self-discovery is a journey, and it comprises a path that is unique to you, with some similar detours we all take along the way. You'll learn about the social science of teaching and how these perspectives influence your role as a teacher. You'll reflect on where you are and where you want to be.

In part 2, we'll shift focus to perspective-taking instructional methods and move from theory to practice. This section is a step-by-step workbook-style approach to perspectives as a lesson-planning framework. Essentially, you'll get an easy-to-follow guide to creating your own plan for any grade level in any subject. As my third grader showed us earlier, elementary students understand perspective. In fact, research tells us that children as young as thirty-six months can understand visual perspective-taking.[2] You'll learn how to tap into your creative teaching capabilities through perspective-getting and use that inspiration to create high-engagement, meaningful, perspective-taking lessons for your students.

Chapters 1 through 3 are titled as questions you will answer through your own exploration. By contrast, in part 2, we do away with the questions and move into action.

In part 2, we focus on students' roles because we're moving from theory (part 1) to practice (part 2). In chapter 4, we focus on finding new perspectives for planning learner-centered role-play activities. These are the lesson lenses in the appendices. In chapter 5, I explain how to connect a lens to a role-play activity. This is a great way to brainstorm creative, dynamic lessons. Finally, in chapter 6, we put it all together with my step-by-step guide so you can create your own Lenses Plan.

Let's get started!

PART 1
YOUR ROLE

1

WHO ARE YOU?

> *The unexamined life is not worth living.*
> — SOCRATES —

The Teacher-Type Quiz

Considering my obsession with roles, you probably won't be surprised by my affinity for personality quizzes. I'll never forget ripping open a copy of *Teen Vogue* to take them! As silly as it sounds, the idea is rather intriguing. I answered multi-choice questions about myself, and then my answers revealed my "boy band personality type."

Personality quizzes are assessments designed to measure personality patterns people universally exhibit. They attempt to reveal roles we inherently assume based on our personality traits. At best, they provide insight into our categorical social behaviors, which, in turn, can help us adapt to different situations. At worst, they're completely wrong and good for an innocent laugh.

The quizzes you find online may be nonscientific. Unless administered by a professional or professional organization, you can't guarantee they are reliable (producing the same results for the same person if taken more than once) or valid (testing what they say they are testing). Nevertheless, they are wildly popular.

For example, the Enneagram Institute, created in 1997 by Don Richard Riso and Russ Hudson, "was formed to further research and development of the Enneagram, one of the most powerful and insightful tools for understanding ourselves and others."[1] Recently, Enneagram has taken social media by storm. You'll find social media accounts with hundreds of thousands of followers dedicated to posts about each Enneagram personality type. I even saw one that likened Disney princesses to different Enneagram personality types.

With a quick internet search, you'll find personality quizzes that test your level of introversion, your love language, and your leadership style. Click through BuzzFeed, and things really start to get interesting. If you're feeling introspective, you can discover your school lunch stereotype, which cartoon cat you are, and your best breakup song.[2]

There is a reason BuzzFeed and other websites keep churning out these over-the-top quizzes. They get clicks, lots and lots of clicks, and I think I know why. If you look past their pop-culture exterior (and well-crafted clickbait titles), these magazine-style personality quizzes are hyper-engaging. Why? Well, they reveal some truths about personality, and even when they don't, they provide a vessel for self-reflection.

"This is ridiculous! I'm not lazy, like Garfield! I'm sweet, like Hello Kitty!"

These quizzes provide an easy and fun way to reflect on our behaviors, personality traits, and likes and dislikes. So if teachers are a special type, why not give it a try for ourselves? These questions aren't scientific but are meant to open the door to the pathway of self-discovery.

Let's give it a try. Mark your best answer to the ten questions below.

Question 1: Which characteristic do you most look for in a friend or partner?

- A. Someone who is fun
- B. Someone I can talk to
- C. Someone who makes me laugh
- D. Someone who tells a great story
- E. Someone who has the same interests as I do

Question 2: What is your perfect weekend activity?

   A. Watching movies or TV. My best ideas come from pop culture.
   B. Attending a book club meeting. I love connecting with other bibliophiles.
   C. Going to a show. Entertain me!
   D. Attending a dinner party. There are so many good stories to hear.
   E. Reading. My favorite quote is, "Never stop learning."

Question 3: What is your favorite movie/TV genre?

   A. Whatever's trending. I love knowing what's cool.
   B. Biopics. I love learning about people's lives.
   C. Sitcoms. I love a good laugh.
   D. Dramas. I love a good story.
   E. Documentaries. I love anything by Ken Burns.

Question 4: Which of the following most closely describes how you plan a lesson or unit?

   A. I create a detailed plan, then pore over the details until it's perfect.
   B. I think about my students' social and emotional learning needs first and plan my instruction around that.
   C. Plan? What plan? I'm all about improvising. Sure, I have an idea in mind, but the best lessons come from the moment.
   D. I have a general plan, but I'm really good at talking my way through the lesson.
   E. I let the content drive the plans. I spend time studying the content so I'm ready to deliver.

Question 5: Which of the following is the best indicator of a successful lesson?

   A. My students are highly engaged in the activity.
   B. My students have a chance to reflect, discuss, and build community.

C. My students laugh and enjoy themselves.
D. My students ask a lot of questions.
E. My students learn the content.

Question 6: Which activity would you be most likely to do in your classroom?

A. A classroom transformation complete with costumes, music, and decor
B. Small-group or one-on-one conferencing so I can speak to every student
C. A role-play activity in which students have to show what they know on the spot
D. A teacher-led whole-class discussion so I can direct the conversation with my information but give the students a voice as well
E. A structured lab in which students follow steps to explore a phenomenon in my content area

Question 7: Which of the following is your preferred way to deal with disruption in the classroom?

A. I downplay the issue and know we'll move on to the next activity shortly.
B. I talk privately to the student or students to address the disruption after the fact.
C. I keep it light and fun to shift the focus from the behavior; students can usually tell when I'm serious, though.
D. I make a call home to describe what happened and discuss a solution.
E. I reiterate the expectations and model the appropriate behavior.

Question 8: How do you contribute to your professional community?

 A. I plan and present at workshops and PD at my school and beyond.
 B. I mentor others, informally or formally, in my district.
 C. I have a great online presence in teacher communities.
 D. I share whatever I can with colleagues and other teachers.
 E. I write professionally to share the latest research.

Question 9: Which of the following statements best describes your biggest strength as a teacher?

 A. I'm great at coming up with innovative ideas and initiatives.
 B. I'm great at forming good relationships with students.
 C. I'm great at getting students excited to learn.
 D. I'm great at communicating my content.
 E. I'm great at knowing my content.

Question 10: Where could I improve my teaching practice?

 A. I get so caught up in the lesson planning that I have a hard time keeping up with feedback.
 B. I want students to know I'm there for them, but I sometimes need clearer expectations and boundaries.
 C. I could work on getting better organized in planning and prep so I don't always have to rely on my personality.
 D. I enjoy giving a great lecture, but I should work on changing up the style once in a while.
 E. My content is the driving force in my class, but I could work on ensuring my instruction aligns with student goals.

When you're done, tally up your responses. How many As, Bs, Cs, Ds, or Es did you get? Are you seeing any patterns?

If you answered mostly As, raise your hand because you are the host teacher type:

As a host teacher type, you are the life of the party—*ahem*—classroom. Just like the host of a murder mystery dinner or a marvelous masquerade ball, you understand the dynamics of the classroom. You captivate with creativity and dazzle with design. You'll sparkle in the spotlight but have no problem passing the mic when the time is right. Everyone wants an invitation to this classroom party!

Personality Pitfalls: Whenever something calls for a party (or an exciting lesson), you pick up the phone and start to put things in motion, even when you know you might not have the time, energy, or resources to get it done. You usually make those wild ideas come to life, but you'll be utterly exhausted afterward. If you're not careful, you'll go from being the life of the party to the party pooper.

If you answered mostly Bs, you're the nurturer teacher type:

As a nurturer teacher type, you are a warm security blanket for kids to come to, offering comfort amid the chaos of the classroom. Sometimes, they'll look to you for advice or a shoulder to cry on. Most often, they come to your classroom knowing you'll always have kindness, understanding, and a close-knit classroom community. By nature, you're a careful listener and caring cheerleader.

Personality Pitfalls: Your nature is to nurture, which makes it hard for you to practice tough love. You're a giver, but you must set boundaries and remind yourself, "Don't be a pushover." If you give them all an inch, some may take a mile. If you're too consumed with charity, you might find your kindness mistaken for weakness.

If you answered mostly Cs, you're the comedian teacher type:

As a comedian teacher type, you're kind of like a farmer: you're outstanding in your field. (Get it?) Of course, you're a fan favorite in the classroom. Scholars love a teacher who can make them holler (aka *laugh*—my weak attempt to be funny). Humor is a universal language, and you're a wizard of the wisecrack, a wordsmith of the witty. You stir them with satire and show them that learning should be fun.

Personality Pitfalls: You can dish out a joke, but can you take one? Kids can be comedians, too, but they often lack the tact to know when to spit and when to quit. How well you deal with hecklers can make or break your set. If you can't keep your cool, you might struggle to soften a tough classroom crowd.

If you answered mostly Ds, you're the storyteller teacher type:

As a storyteller teacher type, you have a gift for the gab. Students love gathering around your classroom campfire to hear a sensational story or a tantalizing tale. You flourish with the figurative. No matter the topic, you can come up with an allusion or analogy to capture their concentration.

Personality Pitfalls: A story loses its luster if it has too many details, and you've been known to over-tell a time or two. Even the most magical narrative can be drowned out by student snores. If you can't carefully craft your anecdote, you risk being branded as boring.

If you answered mostly Es, you're the scholar teacher type:

As a scholar teacher type, you inspire with information. You are like an erudite encyclopedia for your expertise. Students admire your spirit for scholarship, and it impassions their inquiry on your subject. You don't need fancy plans; you know your subject like the back of your hand.

Personality Pitfalls: You love your subject so much it's hard to see why some students don't, and you can take it a bit personally when their knowledge and interest run dry. If you don't plan, you risk placing passion before pedagogy.

The Results

How did I do? Was I right about who you are, or are you scratching your head in disbelief? Are you ready to argue about how wrong I was? Was I right, at least in part?

These questions are a good way to begin teacher self-reflection. In truth, you're probably a combination of these roles and many others not mentioned. Maybe this quiz offered you a look into your teacher-type tendencies, but it's only a narrow view of what makes you who you are.

In truth, I created these roles based on teacher stereotypes—some observed in real-life encounters and some imagined from media and film. Although this can be a fun topic of conversation at a staff meeting, I know just as well as you do that we, as educators, are far more complex than being reduced to a single role.

So then, what's the point?

We literally just did a role call. That's r-o-l-e, or a part or character assigned or taken on, as in your teacher type in the classroom.

The phrase you're more familiar with is *roll call*, which dates to the thirteenth century. It comes from the word *role*, meaning a scroll or rolled-up piece of paper. Later, in the 1590s, the word was associated with the military. To call roll was meant to determine who was present.[3] That brings us to the roll call we do (or forget to do) every morning in our own classrooms.

The roll call tells us who is present in body, but it is the *role call* that tells us who is present in body *and* mind.

The role call can also give us insight into ourselves: the roles we assume intentionally and unintentionally. Equipped with a better understanding of ourselves, we can make classroom choices that best align with our authentic teaching selves.

Every day, when we step into our classrooms, we assume a role, and if we're lucky, our students try out roles as well. But we don't need to rely on luck. There is a way to create meaningful activities that increase student engagement and learning, and it all begins with the power of perspective.

The Power of Perspective

You wake up in the middle of a small room. The room is empty except for a small bed and chair. There is an opening at the front of the room. When you approach the opening, you're met with a bright light shining at you, casting your shadow on the back wall. You try to look out of the opening, but it's blinding, disorienting.

What do you do? Do you leave and enter the uncertainty of whatever awaits you on the other side? Or do you retreat farther into the room, enveloping yourself in the predictability and safety of what you can perceive?

In the late eighteenth century, philosopher Jeremy Bentham asked these same questions. He surmised that with a skewed perspective, one would give in to fear of the unknown and remain in the safety of the room. The result was the panopticon.[4]

The panopticon was a blueprint for a prison that Bentham designed while visiting his brother in Russia. Here, Bentham observed a unique style of worker observation: his brother sat in the center with workers arranged around him.[5]

The panopticon functions like this: In the center of a large circular building is a high watch tower that projects light into the surrounding rooms. An inspector sits in the center and can look into the cells anytime, but the prisoners can't see the inspector. They never know if they're being watched.

Bentham's model uses principles of surveillance and perspective to create an omnipotent presence. The word *panopticon* comes from the Greek παν- "all" and -οπτικος "seeing." In theory, Bentham believed the inspector wouldn't have to watch every prisoner at once; in fact, he couldn't. The fact that they *could* be observed at all times was all that mattered. Though never fully brought to fruition, Bentham's theory demonstrates the power of perspective.

You might find it ironic that we're starting with a description of a prison in a book about teaching. However, architecturally and even structurally speaking, school buildings often follow a prison model: long halls with branched-off classrooms, closed doors, and bells to signal movement.[6] This perspective concept wasn't new even during Bentham's time, and it doesn't have to be centralized around a physical prison. It's a theme that has been explored again and again in philosophy, social theory, literature, and film.

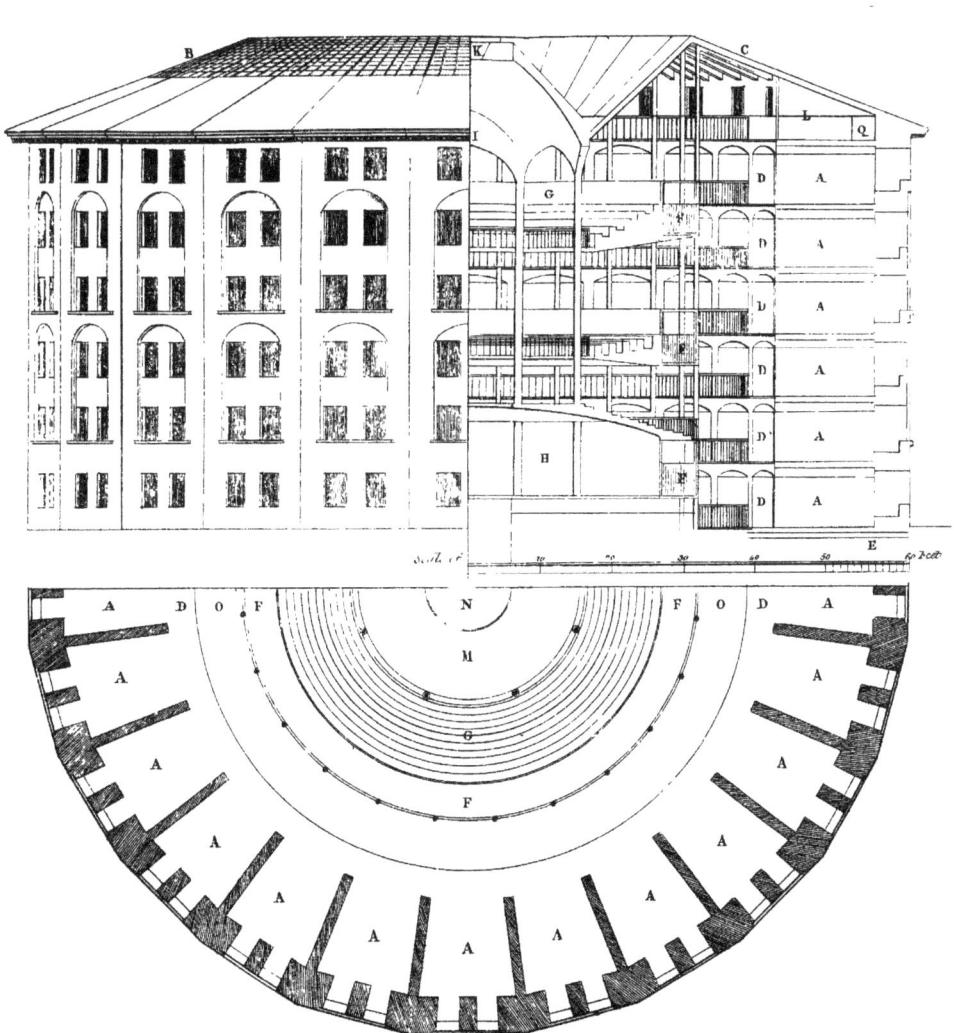

Plato's *Allegory of the Cave* provides one of the most foundational examples of the power of perspective.[7] Chained to a wall in a cave, a group of people spend their lives facing a blank wall, their perspectives shaped only by shadows of the outside world. To them, this is the world. When a prisoner breaks free, he observes the room, the fire casting shadows on the wall and strange objects casting the shadows. Overcome with fear and disbelief, he retreats to the wall with his fellow prisoners, his singular, safe perspective restored. He would rather live in a false reality than broaden his perspective.

But, if perhaps the freed prisoner is dragged out of the cave and forced to take in the world around him, he will soon learn that the real world, although unusual and unforgiving, is so much better than his existence in the cave.

In essence, this is the goal of education: to draw someone out of the dark and into the light of truth and knowing. To break it down even further, the prefix *e-* means "out," the Latin root *duc* means "to lead," and the suffix *-ation* means "the action of doing something."

Therefore, *education* literally means the act of leading out into a world of new perspectives.

Perspective and Perception

Though they are close cousins, perspective and perception are not interchangeable. *Perspective* is a cognitive process for seeing an object, event, or situation from a particular angle, while *perception* is more personal. It's your cognitive *and* emotional view of the world around you. These distinctions are subtle but important. The problem is that your perceptions can be deceiving.

Let's start with your perception of things that happened in the past.

Recently, I enjoyed rewatching *Star Wars: Episode V - The Empire Strikes Back* with my own kids for the first time. I thoroughly enjoyed quoting the most iconic line to them and promptly had them repeat it.

You probably know it well. Darth Vadar and Luke Skywalker are lightsaber-dueling when Darth Vader says, (Can you fill in the blank?).

Of course, you can! Everyone knows Darth Vader says, "Luke, I am your father."

I saw this movie many times and have repeated this phrase over and over with much gusto since I was a child.

If I were a contestant on *Jeopardy* and the final clue was "this is what Darth Vadar famously says to Luke in *Star Wars: Episode V - The Empire Strikes Back*," I would have gone all in and confidently written, "What is 'Luke, I am your father'?"

And, yet, I would have been wrong.

Yes, you read that right. That is not what Darth Vader says. He actually says, "No. I am your father."

Um, what? If you're reeling with this news, I can assure you I was too (and still am). How could this be? How could this happen?

Well, first, let it be known that according to *The New Yorker*, this line is the most misquoted movie line of all time.[8] How have so many people gotten this wrong over and over?

The answer is the Mandela effect.

The Mandela effect got its name from Fiona Broome, a self-proclaimed paranormal researcher who famously recalled the death of Nelson Mandela. The problem was that Mandela wasn't dead. Broome realized thousands of people had the same (false) shared memory of Mandela dying in prison in the 1980s, although he lived until 2013.[9]

Although some conspiracy theorists attribute this phenomenon to alternative universes, psychology has a better answer. When we remember something, our brains activate neurons in a process called *reconsolidation*. This means that our brains are constantly retrieving and rewriting memories as we gain new experiences and learn new information. In doing so, some memories are altered, which can lead to confabulation, or the creation of a false memory.[10]

Think back to your first year of teaching, or if you're a preservice teacher, your first year of high school. No matter how long ago this was in the past (for some of us longer than others), whatever you're thinking right now is probably wrong.

Blunt, I know, but it's true. Consider this blunder as an example. For years, I thought back fondly to my very first classroom. I pictured student desks in a U shape, book posters that adorned the walls, and my desk in the front corner by the door. Proud of myself for my superb memory, it wasn't until I found a picture of my actual first classroom over ten years later that I caught a significant confabulation. I was picturing the wrong classroom! It finally dawned on me that I moved to a new classroom after my first year, and that second classroom was the one I remembered when I thought back to my first year of teaching.

I created a false memory of my first year of teaching in the wrong classroom! What else was I unintentionally inventing? It makes sense, though. Try to recall what you ate for lunch two days ago or a week ago. If you do a little investigation into your special year, I'm confident you'll find a confabulation of your own.

Unfortunately, our perceptions about how we'll feel in the future aren't much better. This concept is called *prospection*. Daniel Gilbert, a professor of psychology at Harvard University, explains this phenomenon in his book *Stumbling on Happiness*.[11] Gilbert explains we look forward to events in the future with more excitement than the happiness we experience when they happen.

For example, the pleasure you get from *looking forward* to summer break is often a lot more than the happiness you *have* on summer break. I've experienced this many times. When we're in the dark days of January, I love thinking about how amazing that warm sun will feel when I'm basking in it on our annual summer vacation to the beach.

What I don't daydream about is how stressed I'll be with a crying baby who missed his nap and just stuffed a handful of sand in his mouth. Going to the beach with a baby isn't all that fun, but we do it anyway! Why? Well, we love having something to look forward to, and

I can admit that I'm frankly terrible at predicting what will be fun in the future based on what sounds fun right now.

On the flip side, when we worry about how bad something will be in the future, it seems much worse than it ends up being in reality. This is the essence of anxiety, after all. I'll never forget how nervous I was for my first classroom observation. I couldn't enjoy my brother's Friday night football game, and I had an awful case of the Sunday scaries. But guess what? When the time came, I did the lesson, and the world didn't shatter. Afterward, I realized my nerves over the observation were much worse than the lesson itself.

There is a psychological explanation for our errors of perception, and the culprit is our brains. As it turns out, running our bodies takes quite a bit of energy. Human brains, for example, make up only 2 to 3 percent of our total body weight but use as much as 25 percent of our energy.[12] For efficiency's sake, our brains use memories and previously learned information to make quick inferences about what will happen next.[13] It uses what we already know to fill gaps in our perceptions (things we haven't experienced yet), ultimately saving us energy.

While this efficiency mechanism works splendidly a lot of the time, that's not always the case. This is where perception meets illusion.

A visual illusion happens when our brains fill in a perception gap and guess wrong. For example, there is a famous road in the little town where I grew up. We called it the road with the tree in the middle. As you may have guessed, when driving down the road, it looks like there is a tree smack dab in the center. You have about fifty feet to panic that you're about to drive into a giant tree trunk before you get close enough to realize the road swerves at just the right downward angle to create the visual illusion. You drive right around that tree. But before you do, your brain fills the visual gap by reporting that it's in the center of the road.

Here's another example:

If you stare at the box long enough, you will likely see gray circles that appear at the white intersections. You might see them, but they aren't there. When perception does not jive with reality, we have an illusion.[14]

While this might seem like bad news for our perception, I haven't told you the good news yet: we have at least some control over perception. Let's look at the duck-rabbit illusion, a famous polystable illusion.

A polystable illusion is a still or moving image that appears to have more than one interpretation. Your brain can only interpret one image at a time, thus creating the illusion of either a vase or two faces looking at each other. Can you see both animals? How long can you see one before flipping to the next? Do you need to look from different angles to perceive the different images?[15]

You may have to really focus, but with the right cues (like the questions I asked above), you can likely make out both images and flip between the two. Researchers have been asking these questions for years, and they have reported that attention and mental control are at least two factors that can help us perceive different interpretations of a visual illusion.[16]

While this is good news in terms of visual perception, attention and mental control aren't enough to lift the veil of illusion. When our brains fill in mental gaps with memories and previously learned information, we can use attention and mental control to perceive visual illusions more accurately. True. But there is one more layer we need to pull back, and it's one we don't realize is there unless we know where to look.

Implicit Bias

Transcendental philosopher Ralph Waldo Emerson suggested looking to nature. He wrote:

> In the woods, we return to reason and faith. There I feel that nothing can befall me in life,—no disgrace, no calamity, (leaving me my eyes,) which nature cannot repair. Standing on the bare ground,—my head bathed by the blithe air, and uplifted into infinite space,—all mean egotism vanishes. I become a transparent eye-ball; I am nothing; I see all; the currents of the Universal Being circulate through me; I am part or particle of God.[17]

Our memories and knowledge systems are always retrieved through an invisible lens of our lived experiences. That means our upbringings, belief systems, friendship circles, and even where we live cloud our "transparent eye-ball" with something brain science calls *implicit bias*.

When our brain makes lightning-quick choices to fill the gap, it uses our biases to categorize and stereotype situations and people quickly. This is all done without our conscious knowledge, hence the term *implicit*. The result is an unconscious tendency away from neutrality and toward prejudice.[18]

As educators working with so many different students on a day-to-day basis, this might feel especially concerning. If we have biases we don't even know are there, how can we avoid unknowingly applying these feelings to our relationships with students?

Fortunately, there is something we can do about it: awareness. Awareness can counter implicit bias when paired with a desire to do better and with interventions to make it happen.[19] One step toward clear perception is to take an implicit bias test from Project Implicit.[20] You can take several Implicit Association Tests (IATs) to discover your unconscious attitudes and beliefs on topics ranging from race to age to body type, just to name a few.

Once identified, we can work to counter our prejudices consciously by taking accountability and seeking new perspectives (more on that to come in chapter 3). Fortunately, this is one area of teaching we are not short on: we get hundreds of unique perspectives from our students.

Of course, as Emerson suggested, we can always take time to immerse ourselves in nature, where we cannot only see but absorb the raw, natural world around us without the push and pull of illusions from our daily lives. Our transparent "eye-ball" is not easy to access, as Emerson laments, but it's not impossible to discover.

Thankfully, our minds are malleable. With attention, mental control, and awareness, we can learn to carefully verify our perceptions with stable reality. Since we know our initial and implicit perceptions can be faulty, it's important we continue to explore and challenge our perceptions, even of ourselves.

Your Perception of You

Let's get back to the central question posed at the beginning of this chapter: "Who are you? Really, who are you?"

I'm not just talking about the few sentences you share when introducing yourself to a group at a professional development gathering. Instead, let's return to the teacher-type roles and reflect on how accurately the role describes you. What is similar? What do you object to? You can take a few minutes to journal, think, or talk with a friend or coworker.

When you're done, let's revisit those questions from the teacher-type quiz. But this time, I'll give you some open-ended cues to help focus your attention on—well—you. Again, you can review them in whatever way works best for you.

1. What characteristics do you most look for in a friend or partner?

   _____
   _____
   _____
   _____

2. What is your perfect weekend activity?

   _____
   _____
   _____
   _____

3. What do you like to do in your spare time?

   _____
   _____
   _____
   _____

4. How do you plan a lesson or unit?

   _____
   _____
   _____
   _____

5. Which classroom activities are you most likely to do?

   _____
   _____
   _____
   _____

6. How do you measure a successful lesson?

   _____
   _____
   _____
   _____

7. How do you deal with disruption in the classroom?

   _____
   _____
   _____
   _____

8. How do you contribute to the professional community?

   _____
   _____
   _____
   _____

9. What are your strengths as a teacher?

_____

_____

_____

_____

10. How could you improve your teaching practice?

_____

_____

_____

_____

There are so many more questions I could ask, but I crafted these particular questions to give you insight into the rest of this book. Understanding ourselves and how we see ourselves is a long and winding road with no destination.

While that can feel awfully scary, it reminds us that we don't have to have it all figured out now—or at any point in our lives. Your perception of yourself—specifically as a teacher and generally as a human—can and should evolve as you travel down the road of life. So if you have some say in who you are, why not explore who you want to be?

2

WHO DO YOU WANT TO BE?

> *And mostly we need to pick and choose*
> *Who we listen to so we follow our own path*
> *Yeah we need to follow our own path.*
> — NIKKI GIOVANNI

I tossed and turned for hours before resigning myself to the fact that I wouldn't get much sleep. It was the night before the first day of school in my second year of teaching. At some point in the year prior, the innocence of my rosy student teaching days slowly slunk away to reveal the reality of an overworked, underpaid first-year teacher.

While I still looked back fondly on my days as an English literature major, I couldn't help feeling a little resentful. As an undergraduate student, I loved attending class with wise English professors and my fellow English majors. We would sit in a big circle and discuss the reading from the night before, everyone eager to defend their interpretations. When I started teaching, I was expecting to re-create the magic of my college English classes. Unfortunately, those intriguing seminar-style literature courses set me up for a major wake-up call when I found myself staring at thirty squirrely sophomores for seven forty-five-minute periods a day. I realized pretty quickly I wasn't going to be able to waltz in and discuss the reading like I assumed my beloved college professors did. That's why I couldn't sleep the night before the first day of year two. What I was planning for day one just didn't feel right. And it wasn't. Having started off too idealistic in my classroom management philosophy, I tried to turn the tables. You know the old teaching adage, "Don't let them see you smile until the second semester"? Well, that was going to be me. It's easier to start tough and soften up than start soft and toughen up, eh? No, I wasn't going to start out laid back. Instead, I was going to be tough. They were going to know I meant business.

Emulating other members of my department, I preplanned a rigid and structured instructional protocol for the first unit and prepared a strict classroom management plan.

It's laughable to think back to my behavior on that first day. Kids are smart. I know they saw right through me.

"This isn't who I am at all," I confessed to my husband, who is also a teacher. It didn't feel right then, and I knew I wouldn't enjoy an entire year of this.

Exasperated, I asked him just to tell me what I should do.

He replied, "You should just be you."

Social Beings

During my first two years of teaching, I was dealing with an incongruent life. According to Todd Rose, author of *Collective Illusions*, an incongruent life is one in which we live in conflict with ourselves. That was me. For at least one school year and the start of the next, I was defying my own personality, morality, and principles by trying to adopt a teaching style that I admired in others but didn't jive with what made me, me.

Sadly, this is a common occurrence, at least among the preservice teachers I work with. It's often easier to adapt to what you see working for others than to pave your own way and risk being different from your colleagues and peers.

Before you beat yourself up over this, you should know there is an evolutionary explanation for this tendency. It's what separates *Homo sapiens* from other animals: we are particularly social beings with a penchant for fiction.

In his book *Sapiens*, Yuval Noah Harari identifies some interesting social patterns that make humans unique.[1] We can cooperate with other humans in impressively large groups. Think about it. Some of us work with over 150 humans (aka students) in one single day, which interestingly is around the threshold for humankind's collaboration capacity. By contrast, the group size for chimps is roughly fifty. In other words, we're far more social than other animals. This isn't just by happenstance.

It is a direct result of our love for stories.

Ancient *Homo sapiens* became great at storytelling to advance groupthink. They used storytelling, in what we now call myths, legends, and fantasies, to pass down their shared values and beliefs from generation to generation. The ability to describe things we've never seen helps us form shared perceptions, which in turn creates tight bonds and helps us work together with so many other people.

In the last chapter, we identified a big problem with conflicting reality (fact) and illusion (fiction). However, the fact that we have the cognitive capacity to understand fiction sets us apart. Corralling and communicating with such a large group requires shared common beliefs.

For example, establishing shared values, expectations, and procedures in your classroom is a foundational classroom management pillar.

We are social beings. While that helped us rise to the top of the food chain, it didn't come without its price. *Homo sapiens* often fall victim to the comparison game.

The Comparison Game

To be a teacher is to stroll into a world of wondrous learning experiences every single day. Well, maybe it's more like powerwalking your way to the restroom during a five-minute break when you can barely spare a quick glance into the other classrooms. But that glance is enough to take note of what's happening in your colleague's classroom. If you're not careful, that glance can become a significant source of the comparison game.

Formally, the comparison game is referred to as social comparison theory (SCT). The term was first coined in 1954 by psychologist Leon Festinger to describe the phenomenon of humans' tendency to compare themselves to others.[2] On one hand, Festinger reported this can be a helpful way to build self-awareness and motivation; however, left unchecked, it can lead to envy, regret, and self-loathing.

It's hard to imagine Festinger could have predicted the implications of SCT in today's social media–dominated world. Studies have overwhelmingly shown that exposure to social media, especially visual platforms, creates an atmosphere of upward social comparison, harming self-esteem and well-being.[3]

With the prevalence of #teachergram and #teachertok, educators are no longer just glancing at their coworkers' classrooms as they move through the school. Rather, they're opening classroom doors to teachers across the world, and as we've learned, perception doesn't equal reality. What we see through the screen is one of the greatest examples of Plato's cave playing out in the modern day. The screen is the cave.

Scrolling through Instagram, Pinterest, Facebook, or TikTok, you'll see picture-perfect classrooms. To beat the comparison game and step out of the cave to meet reality, we must consciously remind ourselves that those images on social media don't show the complete picture. Piles of ungraded essays, a lost lunchbox lying on the floor, a half-finished bulletin board, and a lesson plan that flopped. They're a shadow on the cave wall mimicking reality but not representing it.

Of course, not all aspects of social media are bad. As I reported in a 2020 study,[4] these platforms can open our world to a variety of perspectives that would otherwise be foreign to us. So how do we balance the potential benefits with the known drawbacks? To find value in the escape from reality while also busting the constraints of the screen, you must take up the fight against conformity.

The Fight Against Conformity

Let's say you were given permission to attend a professional development training at a school about an hour away. Your sub plans are ready, you set the GPS to your destination, and you plan to arrive early, maybe with enough time to stop at the nearby Starbucks.

When you get to the school hosting this workshop, you're sent to a classroom and quickly settle in, ready for a day of being a student yourself. The classroom fills up with other teachers, and the presenter gets started.

All is well and good until you see a strange cloud of smoke rising from the vent on the far side of the room. You watch carefully, but everyone else seems to be ignoring it. By now, there is no way they don't see this odorless smoke, and you frantically glance around, wondering why no one seems concerned.

Surely, you would speak up, right?

Research tells us you probably wouldn't.

In a famous 1968 study by John Darley and Bibb Latané,[5] participants completed a questionnaire in a room that quickly filled with smoke. When participants were alone, 75 percent reported the smoke. However, when they were in the same smoke-filled room with planted participants instructed not to act, only 10 percent of participants responded.

The explanation for this surprising conclusion is called the *bystander effect*. In short, it means we are highly affected by those around us; therefore, we closely consider social cues before deciding if we should act.

But that's just one study. What if, instead of the worrisome smoke, you were asked to complete a simple vision test?

This time, you're given a line segment and asked to find its match. That sounds easy! Ah, but I'm sure you've guessed by now, there must be a catch.

In this famous 1956 experiment, Solomon Asch asked participants to match lines, but what he didn't tell them was that there were confederates (someone who is in on a secret the rest of the participants don't know) planted in the room who were instructed to give wrong answers secretly and intentionally.[6] These results indicated that nearly 75 percent of participants conformed to give the wrong answer at least once. That means they knowingly gave the wrong answer to go with the group.

I decided to informally test how strong the pull to conform was with my college students. Before class began, I clued several students in on the plan: during our attendance question roll call, I would ask the class to tell us what 8 x 4 equals. The catch is that I would ask them to say 8 x 4 is 34, not 32, and I would call on them first.

When the rest of the class arrived, I casually said, "Let's do a math fact attendance question." I started by asking my confederate students the question, and they all gave incorrect answers. Then, I moved on to the rest of the students. Some puzzled, naïve "participants" curiously looked around the room, but I bet you can guess what happened. Every single student gave the wrong answer. Yes, even the math majors.

We laughed about it afterward. A few students admitted they didn't even think about the answer being wrong; they trusted the other students and just repeated after them. Even more said they knew the answer was wrong, but they were confused and figured it was "a joke or something," so they followed the group. This was a good lesson in conformity for all of us.

It is so easy to adapt to what you see around you with little regard for your why, especially in schools. When we're thrown challenge after challenge, following the crowd can become the norm, which (unbeknownst to you) slowly stifles your innovation and defies the role you have in your own classroom.

Conformity and Your Role

Schools are complex places with accepted behaviors, instructional theories, and even social etiquette that can vary from building to building. Consider dress code, for example. You likely have an idea of your school's dress code for students, but what about a dress code for teachers? Even if you do have professional dress expectations, you probably follow the vibes of your colleagues, which creates a campus of standard dress.

I've noticed this more and more as I've supervised student teachers in different districts throughout our county. In some school districts, teachers dress more formally, wearing ties, dress pants, and fancy shoes; in others, jeans and sneakers are common. When I ask my students to find out the dress code restrictions from their cooperating teachers before going into student teaching, many don't know the formal "rules" because they collectively dress like their coworkers.

If you're comfortable with how you dress at work, there doesn't appear to be any direct harm in following these social norms. Though since we're considering who you want to be in this chapter, it's worth noting a 2017 *Psychology Today* article by Wendy Patrick, aptly titled, "Power Role Play: Dressing for Success Makes You Successful." In it, Patrick cites several research studies all pointing to the idea that "dressing for success exudes credibility and instills confidence."[7]

Dress is only the beginning of the role you assume when you walk into the classroom, and it's a superficial measure at that. However you choose to dress for success, you need to be true to your definition of success and self.

From Conformity to Connection

Let's go back to the story about my teacher identity crisis at the beginning of the chapter. In short, I chose instructional and classroom management strategies based on what I superficially saw in others. This may have worked if those strategies had jived with my personality; however, as a complex being, I found myself in conflict with those strategies, thereby making an already challenging job much more difficult.

I pulled through, and perhaps surprisingly, I know precisely how and why. A research study that began in 1938 expertly summarizes the reason. This study is the world's longest recorded longitudinal study, and its insights and secrets were recently published in a highly anticipated *New York Times* bestseller. The book is called *The Good Life* by Robert Waldinger and Marc Schulz.[8]

The Harvard study followed the lives of over seven hundred participants. For over eighty-five years, researchers asked them—and many of their children—thousands of questions about their lives. Contrary to popular beliefs, the researchers discovered the key to a happy life is *not* fortune or fame, diet or weight, career achievement or salary.

Instead, the number one key to a good life is good relationships.

Waldinger and Schulz explain: "Relationships are not just essential as stepping-stones to other things, and they are not simply a functional route to health and happiness. They are ends in themselves."

With so much data, *The Good Life* provides exceedingly strong and varied evidence to support this claim. One man's story stood out to me, and I think it will for you, too. Here's a summary of his story: Leo DeMarco was one of the early Harvard study participants. He attended Harvard University as an undergraduate student and dreamed of becoming a writer and journalist. However, after fighting in WWII, he put his dreams on hold and returned home to Burlington, Vermont, to care for his sick mother. He never achieved his dream of becoming a writer. The end.

If I stopped there, you might think what a sad life Leo must have endured. "How terrible that he was never able to achieve his dream!" you might say. However, his story was far from sad. As a matter of fact, throughout his participation in the study, Leo consistently reported evidence that he had achieved the good life.

It's true that Leo never achieved his dream of becoming a writer. Fortunately, Leo's story didn't end there.

Can you guess what he did instead? He became a high school teacher.

Let me give you the rest of Leo's story: Leo DeMarco was one of the early Harvard study participants. He attended Harvard University as an undergraduate student and dreamed of becoming a writer and journalist. However, after fighting in WWII, he put his dreams on hold and returned home to Burlington, Vermont, to care for his sick mother. He never achieved his dream of becoming a writer. Instead, he became a high school teacher. He taught for 40 years. He had a wife and four children whom he loved and adored. He also had connections with other teachers and hundreds of students whom he taught and mentored over the years. These relationships brought him joy, and by all measures, Leo was one of the happiest study participants. He didn't make the most money (far from it). He didn't have fame. He didn't become a journalist. But he had good relationships, lots of good relationships.

That's a much different story, don't you think?

Like Leo, I was (and fortunately still am) surrounded by good relationships, which got me through my rocky start as a teacher. I developed good relationships with colleagues at my school and gained mentors who guided me to better understand who I wanted to be. They also helped me to see that the strategies I observed in their classrooms were intentional and specific to them.

In addition, I had strong family relationships. My mom, dad, brothers, and family members gave me support outside of the classroom.

I met other English teachers through social media and began a group chat to vent about challenges we were all facing in similar lines of work. That group chat is still going strong today!

And, of course, my most important relationship was with my husband, Mike, who had the benefit of being four years ahead of me in his teaching journey. His wisdom, guidance, and support gave me the courage to talk through my challenges and develop policies and practices that made sense for my personality.

His advice to just be myself was exactly what I needed to hear at the time. It gave me permission to drop the tough act and experiment with instructional styles I was passionate about. That didn't mean I fixed everything overnight. I still had a long way to go, but fortunately, I had the support to get there.

It's not always easy to develop good relationships, and it's certainly true that taxing relationships can have the opposite effect. Waldinger and Schulz suggest a "social fitness" test to analyze your relationships and determine if they build you up or pull you down. This is particularly important in a school setting. Seeking mentors, confidantes, and friends in your work circle is wise, unless they're not the kind of relationships that invigorate you. Luckily, there are now virtual ways to connect with educators if your in-person relationships don't provide the support you need.

Developing good relationships is one step to moving away from conformity and toward your authentic self. While your support system can lead you to the path of self-discovery, you must eventually take the road alone.

Your Authentic Self

Now I want to remind you of the question I posed at the beginning: Who do you want to be?

Simply put, the answer is *you*.

Throughout this chapter, we've explored the social perks and pitfalls of being a human. Our social nature created our robust capacity for advanced society, and with it came extreme societal pressures. This is what makes finding your authentic self so challenging. Simply defining *authenticity* poses surprising challenges.

So what does it mean to be authentic? It's not easy to answer, but it's a valiant pursuit. To find our role in the classroom, we must know quite a bit about ourselves and be able to act on what we know without the pressures of perception and illusion.

Why is it so difficult to define? Talk of authenticity is entwined with broader discussions of ethics, self-awareness, subjectivity, and philosophy. Still, in its most general sense, authenticity means being true to oneself. This is likely the definition we all know; nonetheless, it's a vague explanation that doesn't get us any closer to determining how to be our authentic selves, especially in the classroom.

A psychological perspective on authenticity provides more insight, though definitions are often rooted in theory. *Autonomy*, or freedom from control, is a keyword in the social psychology literature. Richard Ryan and Edward Deci explain autonomy as a feeling dependent on a person's perception of their freedom to act and communicate without being influenced by others.[9] To simplify, your view of how free you feel to act and communicate is unique to you.

Based on this idea, William Ryan and Richard Ryan concluded that authenticity is less of a character trait and more of an individualized experience that predicts well-being.[10] So if authenticity isn't so much a character trait that applies to all people, that means we just have to figure out how it applies to us.

Michael Kernis and Brian Goldman can help us do just that. They developed four concepts to help us achieve authenticity: awareness, unbiased processing, behavior, and relational orientation.[11] Let's consider each of these concepts and connect them to what you've learned so far in part 1 of this book.

Awareness

Awareness and desire go hand in hand. To reach the destination of self-actualization, you must start with a desire to question, learn, know, and grow. It means facing the harsh truths about the state of your classroom management and instructional style. You'll need to investigate how your behaviors are impacting your choices.

Some challenges will be out of your control; however, you'll need to look at what is within your control and how you play your role. This step "involves being motivated to learn about such things as one's strengths and weaknesses, goals and aspirations, dispositional characteristics, and emotional states." We started this inquiry at the end of chapter 1 by asking questions about ourselves. The more we can reflect on our behaviors, the better our awareness.

Unbiased Processing

As you learned in chapter 2, we're all born with biases. That doesn't make us wrong or bad; it makes us human. It does mean we need to challenge those biases and processes. We must do this in our classrooms and with ourselves. Although Kernis and Goldman use the term *unbiased processing*, I like to think of this of as honest reflection. Honest reflection means we must check our egos and view our challenges and strengths from an objective point of view.

When you can objectively explain your struggles and successes, you can begin to problem-solve and adjust your behavior. For example, I'm a host teacher, so I'm good at coming up with an idea for a new activity at 8:00 p.m. the night before the lesson. While I love marveling at the result, it's far too easy to ignore the toll it took to pull it off. An honest reflection reveals the often overlooked parts: staying up too late, rushing in the morning, and feeling exhausted afterward.

This quiz was only the beginning. I encourage you to dig even deeper by considering your own biases toward yourself and others.

Behavior

Now that you've become aware of your true self and seek to counter your biases, you must ensure your output aligns with the input. In other words, you must behave in ways honoring your true motives and values.

This is the hard part. Acting of your own volition, free from influence or expectations, isn't easy. Social ramifications may outweigh the good of acting with complete authenticity.

Truth be told, it might not be completely wise. Kernis and Goldman explain, "In such instances, we expect that, at the very least, authenticity will reflect heightened sensitivity to the fit (or lack thereof) between one's true self and the dictates of the environment, and a heightened awareness of the potential implications of one's behavioral choices." Basically, you must consider the social outcomes.

So I'm not telling you to be authentic at all costs—especially if it will jeopardize your job. Certainly not. Instead, go back to your awareness cue. Reflect on how and why your behaviors do or don't align with your authentic self. Then use unbiased reflection to consider how best to move forward. For me, it means making a plan to jot down the new activity idea for the next unit and go to bed on time.

Relational Observation

Who gets to see the real you? This final component reveals the key to happiness we unlocked in this chapter. *Relational observation* means you consider how you can be open, honest, and considerate in your own relationships.

Consider Waldinger and Schulz's social fitness test in the From Conformity to Connection section. Which relationships offer you mutual understanding and openness? As I have experienced, these relationships are necessary to help you understand yourself and be free of the negative feelings associated with criticism.

Who You Are and Who You Want to Be

The answer to the questions that begin chapters 1 and 2 are one and the same: *you*. We're not talking about superficial measures. We're talking about examining and reflecting on what makes you special, unique, and authentic. *That* is the version of yourself you should want to be.

Once you know who you are and who you want to be, you can define your role in the classroom.

3

WHAT IS YOUR ROLE?

> *The role of a teacher is to engineer student success.*
> — HARRY WONG

In 1993, a short article was published in *College Teaching*, a journal dedicated to issues in teaching and learning at the postsecondary level, that led to the debate of a decade and beyond. The article by Alison King was titled "Sage on the Stage to Guide on the Side."[1]

In this article, King coined two instructor roles you've likely heard of in any professional development after 1993. The sage on the stage represents not only a predominant teacher role but also an instructional model. The teacher, a beacon of wisdom, stands behind a podium and imparts knowledge to students through lectures.

We're all familiar with this traditional instructional style because we've all heard lectures—some captivating, some not so much. We've heard them from teachers and probably other adults our whole lives. A lecture is direct. It gets to the point, and it makes a point. But it's not always effective.

If you've ever fallen asleep during a lecture from a teacher or professor, you shouldn't feel too bad. A 2014 study made it clear that lecture falls short as an instructional method.[2] Researchers analyzed the results of 225 studies on instructional methods in STEM classrooms, and they found students in lecture-based courses were 1.5 times more likely to fail than their active-learning counterparts.

King called for instructors to move into the "guide on the side" role to rectify the issues with this teacher-centered instructional mode. Citing constructivist learning theory, which suggests learners should construct their own knowledge to gain understanding, King defined the *guide on the side*: "The professor's role is to facilitate students' interaction with the material and with each other in their knowledge-producing endeavor."

This concept wasn't new in the 1990s. Here's a visual that may offer clarity: You walk into a bank to deposit a check. What do you do? You walk up to the cashier. You hand over your money, and your money is immediately applied to your account balance. Done.

Now, consider your students the cashiers. Instead of money, you hand over your knowledge, and it gets deposited right into their brains. I'm sure you can see the problems here.

In *Pedagogy of the Oppressed,* published in 1970, Paulo Freire argues that this model demeans learners as mere vessels devoid of the ability to think or act for themselves.[3] The instructor holds all the knowledge and power, and the instructor decides if and when the knowledge is imparted to the students. Obviously, this isn't good. But it's the default mode for many teachers because lectures dominated their schooling in high school or college.

In these contexts, it's easy to see that the guide on the side is meant to be an answer to the problems identified with the sage on the stage role. However, the guide on the side has challenges of their own. As Erica McWilliam points out,

> The difficulty with "guiding" or "facilitating" is that it can become, at worst, an excuse for passivity on the part of the teacher after tasks have been allocated . . . we have seen the high ground of "guiding" too easily collapse into passive childminding and worksheet distribution.[4]

This means the guide on the side can easily be on the side but never really guide.

When we pit roles against each other, it becomes a competition. For those of us who do not revel in these types of contentious rivalry, we might find ourselves being more of a "Meddler-in-the-Middle" type as McWilliam suggests. According to McWilliam, Meddlers "provide support and direction through structure-rich activity in which they themselves are highly involved."

Now we're getting somewhere! McWilliam is separating the teacher role from the pedagogical approach. In reality, the debate between sage on the stage and guide on the side isn't really a debate about the teacher's role; it's a debate about instructional methods. You've probably heard other names for the same disagreement: teacher-centered versus learner-centered, passive learning versus active learning, direct instruction versus inquiry-based learning, and so on.

That's a lot of discord! So I'd like to bring your attention back to the quotation at the beginning of this chapter. Harry Wong, a guru in classroom management, says, "The role of a teacher is to engineer student success." Our role isn't a pedagogical strategy. Rather, our role is to use instructional strategies to guide our students along the path of learning to success.

Let's review.

The teacher's role is to engineer student success.

The teacher does this with a pedagogical strategy, such as a lecture, discussion, activity, lab, and so on.

The Tour Guide Teacher

You may have picked up on travel imagery throughout the first half of this book. This wasn't an accident. Thanks to my wonder-filled coauthors of *Keeping the Wonder*, I was prepared with an excellent metaphor to take us on a journey to our role in the classroom. Ashley, Abby, Staci, and I are the self-proclaimed queens of creating education-related alliterative metaphors. This brings me to one of our finest: the tour guide teacher.[5]

A tour guide teacher takes students on a journey through learning.

I know this sounds magical and exciting, but as I admitted earlier, traveling (with or without a baby) isn't all fun and games, and neither is learning. That's why students need a tour guide teacher, someone with a map to lead the way through unexpected roadblocks but who will give them space to explore when the path is clear.

The tour guide is a true teaching role, not an instructional strategy. It gives you the freedom to be who you are while providing you with an aspirational model. Here are the key characteristics of a tour guide teacher from *Keeping the Wonder*:

1. **Passion:** A good tour guide is passionate about their content and teaching others.
2. **Inclusivity:** A good tour guide is dedicated to inclusivity so all people feel "welcome and valued."
3. **Receptivity:** A good tour guide is a good listener, reflective, and open to change.
4. **Flexibility:** A good tour guide can adapt and adjust when necessary.

Notice this description isn't telling you how to teach; it's giving you suggestions for characteristics to embody as a teacher. It's a role you can embrace without losing your authenticity.

In fact, maybe you can best the queens of the alliterative metaphor and come up with a better title. Or you can use one or a combination of the teaching roles Yehuda Baruch describes based on archetypes: judge, salesperson, stand-up comic, emperor, coach, and buddy.[6] The point is, we're not choosing a role that traps us in an instructional style box. We're choosing a role that will help us engineer student success.

(Reverse) Engineering Student Success

Have you ever woken up one sunny day and decided to take a flight to Italy? Chances are you haven't, unless you have a lot more funds to work with than the average teacher. So for the sake of this analogy, let's assume you're working with a teacher budget.

In this case, it's doubtful you would ever wake up and decide to take a trip to Italy. Since we assume you don't have a personal jet, traveling commercially means booking and sometimes rebooking flights, train rides, and car rentals. You'll also need a hotel, and even if you have a passion for wanderlust, you'll need a loose agenda if you want to see anything that requires a ticket.

When you plan a trip to Italy, you start with a destination. Your end goal is a tour of Rome, for example. How will you know if you achieved this? Well, if you can tour the Colosseum, the Roman Forum, the Sistine Chapel, and St. Peter's Basilica, you'll consider the trip a success.

You start to plan months ahead. First, you apply for a passport, which will take a few months to receive. (Good thing you did this early!) Then, you book your flights to coordinate with your arrival at the hotel(s) you chose. You choose which day you want to tour which tourist spots, and you buy tickets.

You read all the best blogs about where to eat and how to dress. You make dinner reservations and map the distance from your hotel to the tastiest gelato in Rome. You shop for comfortable walking shoes and a purse to secure your goods. You spend a week packing, and your luggage is over fifty pounds. You spend another day repacking.

After months of planning and preparation, you're ready to leave for the airport feeling prepared to have a successful tour of Rome.

This plan is what productivity gurus call "reverse engineering" for goal setting. This makes sense, right? It's objectively a logical way to set a goal and achieve it. You start with a goal (to tour Italy), set metrics to measure your success (touring the Colosseum, the Roman Forum, the Sistine Chapel, and St. Peter's Basilica), and you create a plan to achieve that goal (the travel itinerary).[7]

We can use this goal-setting strategy to, as Harry Wong suggested in our opening quotation, (reverse) engineer student success.

Why is it, then, that we often do the exact opposite in the classroom? Grant Wiggins and Jay McTighe had the same question.[8]

They observed that it often goes like this in the classroom: A teacher chooses content, either from a textbook or a given curriculum. Then, the teacher creates lessons to teach the content. Then, the teacher makes an assessment to see if the students learned the curriculum.

Wiggins and McTighe thought this was backward, or rather they wanted to see what would happen if teachers turned this traditional "frontloading" approach around.[9] The result was backward design.

Backward design is not an instructional strategy. Rather, it's a planning framework in which a teacher sets an instructional goal for students.

Then, the teacher creates an assessment to measure if (or to what extent) students met that instructional goal.

Finally, the teacher designs learning opportunities (lessons) to prepare students to meet that instructional goal.

Teachers often use this method for long-term planning, such as developing an entire course or a unit. Yet, it works for smaller learning tasks, such as a single lesson plan.

This format isn't new, per se. McTighe and Wiggins wrote about backward design in their book *Understanding by Design* in 2005. Nevertheless, many educators still plan curriculum around content rather than instructional goals, neglecting to think about desired results or determine acceptable evidence before beginning instruction.

The sage on the stage versus guide on the side debate seems like a colossal waste of time from this perspective. The winner is actually a combination of whatever instructional styles best help students arrive at their instructional goal. (I'm still going strong with the travel metaphor, as you can see!)

This doesn't mean frontloading is wrong. On the contrary, it may just mean frontloading is harder. When we use backward design to set our destination first, we don't need to pick a team, or instructional style, and we certainly don't need to debate which style is best. We need to choose an instructional style that will help our students meet their goals, and we can do that with backward design.

So let's set our destination.

Travel opens our eyes to people, places, and perspectives other than our own. It creates an internal capacity for learning we never knew existed. As a tour guide teacher, you will engineer your students' success by opening their eyes, ears, and hearts to new views and worldviews. You'll give them perspective.

Perspective-Taking

Since we're talking about travel, we're going to start with a study of a mountain. Imagine you're looking at three mountains. If a friend went and stood in a location under one mountain, do you think you could guess her vantage point of the others?

It sounds like a pretty easy task, right? And it might be, unless you're under six years old, that is.

In 1956, Swiss psychologists Jean Piaget and Barbel Inhelder published a famous study called the Three Mountain Task.[10] Using a model of three mountains on a table, the researchers set a doll in a unique spot and asked children to determine the doll's perspective from a different vantage point.

They discovered that children age four and under struggled to identify the doll's perspective and instead gave their own. By age six, children could begin to see perspectives outside of their own, and by ages seven and eight, children could consistently identify the correct perspective.

If you've spent any time around a toddler, you know why it's so important they eventually develop this skill. Toddlers are little tyrants!

They demand what they want when they want it, and the worst is when they don't even know what they want. They'll cry, scream, and flail if they don't get it, and they don't give a second thought to how you feel. We don't call them "threenagers" for nothing!

Obviously, this is all anecdotal. However, solid research suggests that the ability to consider how someone else thinks or feels, also known as perspective-taking, is one of the most important social skills. *Forbes* says it's a key leadership skill.[11] *Entrepreneur* writes about the importance of perspective-taking to develop compassion in the workplace.[12] *EducationWeek* suggests it's a foundation for developing empathy.[13]

Formally, academic scholarship indicates perspective-taking builds critical thinking skills, altruism, empathy, open-mindedness, and resilience, and reduces prejudice.[14,15,16,17,18]

Perspective-taking, then, is a desired interpersonal skill and employability skill. You probably already knew that. Why? Because it's blatantly obvious when someone lacks this skill, and there seems to be an abundance of people who do.

Have you ever met someone you thought was selfish, narcissistic, or single-minded? I'm certain you have. But if perspective-taking is so important, why is it so underused?

Well, for one, it's hard. Take this exercise as an example:

Look at the picture of this woman and try to imagine her perspective. What is she thinking? What is she experiencing? Write a few sentences with this sentence starter: The woman in the picture is sitting at the computer, looking out the window . . .

_____

_____

_____

_____

Your response might go something like this:

> *The woman in the picture is sitting at the computer, looking out the window and daydreaming about her upcoming wedding. She can't focus on the essay she's supposed to be writing for the final of her master's degree. Worry begins to creep in as she thinks about how she's going to get it all done. Getting married, graduating, starting a new career—it's a lot.*

Or how about something like this?

> *The woman in the picture is sitting at the computer, looking out the window and thinking about the baby she just left for the first time. She's supposed to be working on invitations for her best friend's upcoming wedding, but she can't stop wondering if the baby (and babysitter) are getting along all right without her.*

Or maybe something like this?

> *The woman in the picture is sitting at the computer, looking out the window and thinking about a brilliant idea that just came to her for a new short story. The happenings outside don't even register as the story unfolds in her mind. A sense of calm comes over her as she plans the first line.*

Was yours something like mine?

It doesn't matter because I have no idea what this woman is thinking or feeling, and neither do you. That doesn't mean this exercise was a waste of time. For one, it's a great creative writing exercise. More importantly, it demonstrates some critical considerations about perspective-taking.

For one, there are actually two types of perspective-taking: 1) imagining how someone else feels and 2) imagining how you would feel in their position. These are two similar concepts, but they each have significant implications.

Let's go back to the exercise above. When you wrote your perspective-taking paragraph, was it at all infused with your personal experience?

Mine absolutely was. I can pick out several instances of how I would feel in the scenario. A mom with a baby? That's me. Someone who writes short stories? Yep, me too. Someone who graduated, landed a new job, and got married within a year? Sounds familiar.

If you did the same, it's something essential to notice. Researchers studied this concept and found that when we attempt to think about *how we would feel* in someone's situation, it's common to experience distress, which can create egotistical motivation. On the contrary, if you just imagine *how someone else feels*, you're more likely to experience empathy, thus creating altruistic motivation.[19]

Our exercise above is not diagnosing you with egotism (not to worry), but it does show us how easy it is to infuse ourselves into someone else's point of view without even realizing it. Even when we attempt to perspective-take with good intentions, we can still get it wrong.

Tal Eyal, Mary Steffel, and Nicholas Epley explain this realization with an important study titled "Perspective-Taking Doesn't Help You Understand What Others Want."[20] They studied a varied group of 2,816 participants across twenty-five experiments. They studied complete strangers and romantic partners, and the results held:

"Perspective-taking may indeed work some wonders, but increasing insight into another's mind does not seem to be among them."

The researchers explain the key is not perspective-taking; it's perspective-getting.

Perspective-Getting

At my wedding shower, we played a game called "How Well Do You Know the Bride?" But there was a creative twist. My aunt, who graciously threw my bridal shower, asked me twenty questions about myself. Here are some sample questions to give you an idea:

- How many kids (if any) do you want?
- What is your favorite color?
- What superpower would you want?
- What animal would you be?
- What's your greatest weakness?

Then, rather than asking the audience to see how many they would get right about me, she asked my soon-to-be husband. On our shower day, she asked our friends and family to guess how many Mike got right out of twenty. Then she read the answers.

What I didn't realize at the time is that my aunt was not only giving me the gift of a good laugh at my wedding shower, she also gave us the gift of perspective-getting. Although some of the responses were silly, others gave us things to talk about that we hadn't addressed otherwise. He thought I wanted five kids, but I wanted three. (We ended up with three.)

The point is that perspective-getting means learning something new about the person. And the easiest way to do it is simply to ask.

It may sound silly that the big strategy revealed in this section is asking; however, it's surprisingly underutilized. In a study called "The Benefits and Obstacles to Perspective-Getting," researchers found that only 26 percent of participants asked for someone's perspective when tasked with predicting how the person would feel when given a particular monetary gift.[21]

The researchers identified a few potential reasons for this that are relevant to our role as tour guide teachers. One reason could be that when people believe they have similarities with someone, they don't think they need to ask. In addition, people generally think they are better at perspective-taking than they are.

Perspective-taking is vital to all sorts of skills for people of all ages, specifically those over six years old who can begin to see perspective. It's also hard, and most of us aren't good at it. To do better, we should transform perspective-taking into perspective-getting, which requires us to overcome our bias, knowledge gaps, and overconfidence by learning, listening, and asking questions.

This wish list (learning, listening, and asking questions) sounds a lot like the learning outcomes we hope for in any classroom with students of any age. This is where our goals (and roles) as instructors intersect with the goals (and roles) we have for our students.

If our goal is to teach students perspective-taking, we must provide learning opportunities for them to engage in perspective-getting. Fortunately, in an educational setting, there is a tried-and-true way to make this a reality: role-play.

Role-Play

Pretend Play

One of my favorite activities as a child was playing school with my two younger siblings. I, of course, played the role of the teacher, and my brothers (and sometimes the neighbors) were my pupils. Mikey, the stereotypical middle child, always played the teacher's pet, who loved pulling pranks with whoopie cushions and disappearing pencils.

Did this prepare me for my future role as a teacher? Maybe, but probably not for the reason you think.

Pretend play is a creative activity that engages children in open-ended learning. It encourages the practice of cognitive abilities related to creative thinking.[22] It requires storytelling, problem-solving, conflict resolution, and brainstorming. Therefore, playing school with my brothers probably helped in the same way that playing Barbie, shipwreck, store, and camping did.

It's doubtful that playing teacher prepared me to deal with pedagogy and classroom management (although I certainly have learned a thing or two from my mischievous brother); still, it may have helped me develop creative thinking abilities, which have certainly been put to the test as a teacher.

Pretend play is a complex study because there are so many outside factors that may impact a causal relationship between pretend play and creativity. Consequently, researchers have pointed out that more clarifying evidence is needed to understand the relationship between creativity and pretend play.[23] Despite these challenges, the researchers clearly advocate for child-centered classrooms instead of teacher-centered, lecture-style classrooms, especially for young children.

Pretend play is the very beginning of developing perspective-getting skills. The benefit is that pretend play can lead children to role-play, which is the key to perspective-getting. Role-play is a pedagogical activity that simulates a person in a unique setting and circumstance. Interestingly, there are two kinds of role-play: 1) role-play in education and 2) role-playing games.

Role-Play in Education

Let's begin with role-play in education. Role-play in education is an active-learning, learner-centered instructional method that promotes high engagement, motivation, and collaboration between learners.[24] If there were ever a sentence that included more educational keywords, I'd like to know. But it's for good reason. Role-play in education is a solid instructional strategy.

Role-play in education can take on many forms. It can be a drama-based activity that mimics the role of actors in a workshop. Or, it can be entirely technology-based, in which case the role-play takes place in a virtual environment.[25] The key is that role-play in education includes some form of simulation of a real-world or fictitious scenario.

Here are some examples:

Students in a third-grade classroom participate in a hot-seat discussion in which one student plays the role of an author and the class plays the press.

Students in an eighth-grade social studies class participate in a mock convention in which students take on roles as candidates, campaign organizers, and voters.

Students in a high school physics class participate in a catapult creation activity in which students take on the role of a team of engineers.

Students in a college education class participate in a mock IEP in which students take on the role of educators and advocates.

Role-Playing Games

Role-playing games (RPG) share scenario-based simulation with educational role-play, with added elements of gamification. This means RPGs have player(s), game master(s), and game rules (also known as a game framework). An RPG uses a storyline and narrative as a scenario, which requires players to complete a quest or accomplish a task to win. Here are some examples:

One of the best examples in schools is an educational escape room. In one of my favorite educational escape rooms, I (the game master) pretend to be interrupted (and embarrassed) by a phone call during a typical presentation. Using the element of surprise, I let the "phone call" play for students and reveal a recording that asks them to help solve the mystery of William Shakespeare's stolen First Folio. Rushing around the room to collect clues and solve puzzles, students become detectives to rescue the artifacts.

Another example is an RPG that anyone can play via Google Earth: Where on Earth Is Carmen San Diego: The Crown Jewels Caper.[26] This virtual RPG creates a travel-based scenario where players must answer geography-related questions to recover stolen loot.

As you can see, role-play can take on many contexts in any educational setting. Even so, there are aspects that all these contexts have in common. They are a meaningful way to encourage perspective-getting.

Role-Play and Perspective-Getting

Role-play has a long history of clinical use dating as far back as the 1800s.[27] Psychologists, for example, have used role-play in both clinical practice and research. In education, researchers agree that role-play is an effective learner-centered strategy.

Most students agree, according to a 2015 study. Rachel Stevens, a college professor in Melbourne, Australia, surveyed 144 college students to find out their perceptions of a role-play activity in their history class.[28] A large majority found the activity to be meaningful and beneficial. This really isn't surprising considering the similarities between pretend play and role-play and role-play and gamification.

What may be more interesting for our purposes is what Stevens reported from the small group of students (between 7 and 11 percent) who didn't find the activity meaningful. The takeaway was that unpreparedness can hinder students' ability to benefit from role-play. Stevens explained that frontloading content knowledge before the activity could benefit all students.

This case study provides an important point about preparing for a role-play activity. In Stevens's case, she advocates for more student preparedness.

How will you prepare students for their role? The first step to success is careful planning on the teacher's part.

First, students need a safe space where they feel comfortable taking on a new role. This means cultivating a classroom community in which students understand the purpose and value of the activity, their role, and how to prepare for their role.[29]

During your preparation, you must maintain the utmost appropriateness and respect for serious content. This means we should never gamify or trivialize real, serious events with activities that make them seem like play. In other words, we don't want to downplay the events by making them seem fun or easy. In addition to being incredibly disrespectful to real people who went through real struggles, it undermines the value of perspective-getting altogether by giving a false perspective of the reality of a struggle.

There is a sensitive way to plan role-play when we're talking about enslavement, genocide, death, disease, war, poverty, and any other traumatic, violent, or disturbing situation.

For example, asking students to role-play as a biographer, historian, or artist to perspective-get for a presentation or project (versus having them role-play as a historical figure) would be effective *and* appropriate. Role-play activities do not have to include gamification or dramatic reenactment, and in some cases, they absolutely shouldn't.

Furthermore, the goal of a perspective-getting activity isn't for our students to reenact traumatic events. As we learned earlier, the goal for perspective-getting is to understand how someone else feels or felt, not thinking about how you would feel in that situation. It's also valuable to consider whose perspectives our students are investigating. Because perspective-getting can lead to empathy, it's important to avoid facilitating an empathetic response for people who have caused serious harm.[30]

In general, when we're talking about historical figures, the value lies in verb roles rather than noun roles. What I mean by this is that students' roles should be based on an action of analysis, such as a researcher, historian, or biographer, not the historical figure. In her presentation titled "Engagement without the Gimmicks" at the Brave History Conference, Megan Forbes, a history teacher and author, provides further support. She explains, "It's important that we learn to interact with history as ourselves, aware of our own identities, and cognizant of the identities of the students in our communities."[31]

In a moving essay in *Rethinking Schools* titled "'Take These Nametags Off!': Disrupting Poorly Designed Classroom Role-Play," Azizah Curry Iluore elaborates on these reflections:

> We must first remember to center our students' humanity and to plan lessons and activities with each of them in mind. We also must plan for unexpected detours that generate difficult conversations, like those challenging the status quo.[32]

Iluore stresses the importance of designing role-play activities with "students' humanity" at the core of the activity. This means carefully considering the roles we're asking our students to take on. She also mentions another critical factor to consider in the planning and following through in the end: debriefing.

It's essential to provide a distinct line where role-play begins and ends so you and your students can debrief and work through the challenges and nuances of perspective-getting. This is where our tour guide teacher fosters a safe space to invite further exploration with the support of a more experienced traveler.

But our goal isn't to take one trip; it's to take lots of trips. This brings us to our final stop before it's time to put all of this learning into practice: multiple perspectives.

Planning with Perspective(s)

When I was in high school, my grandma gave me a book she thought I would like. Admittedly, I always feel a bit of pressure when I read a book someone recommends for me. Books are highly personal, and we can come to love them in very meaningful ways. If there's an expectation by someone who loves a book that you're also going to read it and love it, I'm always hesitant to take it on. However, this was my beloved grandma, so I couldn't say no.

In this particular case, the book was about a ruthless investment banker and a controlling "family man." *Sounds interesting enough*, I thought, although I was a bit confused why my grandma insisted I read it. I trudged through the first hundred pages or so, worried I was going to disappoint her by giving up on it.

But then things got a little more interesting. The narration changed to a different character. It was a new perspective on the events, and my interest was piqued. The narration continued to change six times through the more than six-hundred-page book, and I reveled in the details as each character added new drama and intrigue to the story. My grandma was right!

The book, *Sins of the Fathers* by British author Susan Howatch, was published in 1980, and it wouldn't have caught my interest had it not been for my grandma. Still, I'll never forget the intrigue in discovering how each narrator brought a new and unique lens to tell the story.

I had all but forgotten about this book until ten years later when I started researching the value of multiple perspectives for my dissertation study during my doctoral coursework. While writing a review of literature on multiple perspectives, I came across a book called *Critical Encounters in Secondary English* by Deborah Appleman.[33]

Appleman suggested using literary theory to introduce multiple perspectives to high school students. Ah ha! I was instantly reminded of *Sins of the Fathers* and how I was impacted by hearing multiple perspectives of a single story.

I realized then and there just how important and impactful it can be to bring multiple perspectives to students. I wasn't alone in this revelation.

In 1990, Rudine Sims Bishop wrote a beautiful metaphor that explains how books are windows to the world and mirrors for reflection:

> Books are sometimes windows, offering views of worlds that may be real or imagined, familiar or strange. These windows are also sliding glass doors, and readers only have to walk

through in imagination to become part of whatever world has been created or re-created by the author. When lighting conditions are just right, however, a window can also be a mirror. Literature transforms human experience and reflects it back to us, and in that reflection we can see our own lives and experiences as part of the larger human experience. Reading, then, becomes a means of self-affirmation, and readers often seek their mirrors in books.[34]

Using texts to introduce students to multiple perspectives is an excellent access point, and it's where I began my research.

As an English literature major, I learned how to analyze texts from multiple perspectives in my coursework, most memorably in Literary Theory. In this class, I learned different ways scholars analyze literature. For example, some theorists read and analyze a text through the lens of an author's life. Others focus on the reader's reaction to the text.

Each literary theory provides a different yet intriguing guide to arrive at the meaning of the text. I learned that considering new and multiple perspectives can open the reader's eyes to new ways of thinking and learning. This is why I chose it as the topic for my 2013 dissertation.

Researchers and teachers have written about using literary theory to introduce students to multiple perspectives for years. Here's a brief selection of my favorite scholarly sources from my dissertation: Scholes in 1985,[35] Schade in 1996,[36] Willinksy in 1998,[37] Sagan in 2003,[38] Golden and Canan in 2004,[39] Troise in 2007,[40] and, of course, Appleman in 2009. If you're interested, all these sources are documented in the resources, or you could read my 2013 dissertation, which synthesized their conclusions and results.

I could go on and on with this list, but I'll stop there. The point is there is a solid research base to suggest that teaching literary theory is a good access point to teach multiple perspective-getting.

After researching this topic for over a decade, I understand better than anyone that literary theory isn't for everyone. If you're not a literary scholar (or even if you are), you probably don't want to take the time to learn these complex literary theories to make them accessible to your students.

But I did, and that's what I've been doing ever since. I started experimenting with literary lenses when I realized how they help English teachers create learner-centered literary analysis activities. The goal was for students to learn to look at literature from new perspectives. Each lens applied to a text is a new opportunity for discussion, role-play, and creative thinking.

As I presented and wrote about this topic, I discovered elementary teachers and content area teachers in math, science, and social studies, for example, have long been infusing multiple perspectives into their planning.[41,42,43,44] My goal soon transformed, transcending the secondary English classroom to create a K–12 multiple perspectives planning framework.

I figured out that if I could reframe the discipline of literary theory to focus on students' learning roles, they would see the benefit of multiple perspective-getting. Using my background in literary theory, I created what I call lesson lenses to help teachers develop lessons that encourage students to "see" learning from different perspectives.

When we use literary lenses, it's usually in English class, and we're usually asking our students to apply the lens to literary analysis tasks related to a text. For example, in my high school English class, I might ask students to analyze *The Great Gatsby* from a feminist lens.

Lesson lenses are different. Instead of giving students a lens and asking them to use it, you, the teacher, will use the lesson lenses to plan engaging, perspective-getting lessons for your students. You will put your students into roles to use the lenses, but you'll never have to teach them the theory of the lens. The students will experience perspective-getting through the activities you create using the lens.

With the Lenses Plan, you can create lessons and units that invite students to question the commonplace, consider multiple perspectives, and take action.

So far we've been exploring you and your role as a classroom teacher. At this point, you have some perspective *on* perspective. Whether you take on the role of a tour guide teacher or you use some other inventive metaphor, you have the knowledge to guide your students on a path to valuable learning experiences.

In the second half of this book, I invite you to join me on a journey to bring planning with perspective to your classroom quickly and effectively.

PART 2
YOUR STUDENTS' ROLES

4

FIND YOUR NEW PERSPECTIVE(S)

One of the best parts of the Lenses Plan is that there are hundreds of new perspectives to be discovered! Each lesson or unit is another opportunity to learn new perspectives. While that revelation can feel freeing, it's helpful to have a list of go-to lesson lenses to streamline the lesson-planning process.

In this section, I'll explain my favorite lesson lenses. *With a little help from my friends*, I'll give you ideas and real classroom examples so you can see how they all *come together* in *a day in the life* of a teacher. Carrying on with our travel theme, here's your *ticket to ride* into the Fab Four.

The Fab Four

Inspired by my love for the Beatles (Have you caught the Beatles references in this book?), the Fab Four (lenses) are the four main perspectives that can be used repeatedly with just about *any* lesson. Just like you can find a Beatles song for any occasion, the Fab Four is a great starting point for planning. You likely use these four lenses during your lesson planning without even thinking of it.

As we explore the Fab Four, think about ways you use, or could use, each lens with your classes.

BIOGRAPHY LENS

A biography lens requires us to consider the life and legacy of key figures related to our content. Unlike the other Fab Four literary lenses you'll read about next, the biography lens isn't linked to a specific literary philosophy. Rather, a biography lens is an approach to content analysis. Readers, for example, naturally question the author's intentions and influences when trying to find meaning in the story.

From casual readers to literary scholars, people want to know why an author wrote what she wrote. This instinct is why the biography lens is one of our Fab Four. It transcends literature. In more general terms, people love knowing about people. We like looking up the spouse of the actress in our new favorite movie. We want to know who Jude is in the Beatles' "Hey Jude." We have to know if that couple on HGTV broke up. We're naturally nosey, so we might as well take advantage of this for the classroom.

In the classroom, I bet you use this lens fairly often. Here are some examples for different content areas and grades:

1. In an ELA class, you may tell students about the life of Barbara Park while reading *Junie B. Jones*.
2. In health class, you might talk about Jonas Salk when discussing vaccines.
3. In math class, you may explain who Pythagoras was when teaching the Pythagorean theorem.

Why It Matters

Understanding the perspectives of people involved with your topic is an extremely empowering and eye-opening endeavor. You may discover someone's inspiration or process, which can provide insight into the topic. You may find that sometimes, even the people directly involved with the topic don't agree.

> **Teacher Feature** Mike Rawls is an elementary librarian who is a master at planning with a biography lens. When you scroll through his Instagram account, you'll find wonderful resources highlighting the lives of diverse authors, illustrators, and key figures. Not only is Mike an excellent resource for educators to find books that celebrate cultural diversity, but he also uses a biography lens with his students. For example, his first graders explore the lives of illustrators and how their style contributes to the storytelling. You can learn more about Mike and find hundreds of resources and examples on his Instagram @thebookwrangler.

FORMAL LENS

A formal lens is used anytime you focus on the key points of your content. This lens was inspired by formalism, a school of literary criticism that relies on the work's form to find meaning. In the classroom, a formal lens looks like traditional content learning: studying vocabulary, identifying themes, and memorizing formulas.

I know you use a formal lens because textbooks love a good, formal overview of the content. As a teacher, you need this lens to provide background details that students need to be, well, formally taught.

Here are some examples of how you may use a formal lens in any class or content area:

1. When you teach students Tier 3 vocabulary words—words that are specific to our subject and content—you are using a formal lens. You must teach these words because they are not part of our everyday conversations, and context clues don't really help students decipher their specialized meaning. Examples of Tier 3 words includes factorization, thesis, acidic, osmosis, and clavicle.
2. If you ask students to close read a passage or page, you are using a formal lens. Close reading happens anytime you ask students to read purposefully so they understand a particular text element. Close reading can be assigned for any text or performed orally through a teacher-led read-aloud.

Why It Matters

A formal lens is linked to a traditional exploration of content. Therefore, it's one of the most accessible lenses to add to your planning process. It provides a great access point to set the stage for other lenses. Once students understand the text through a formal lens, you can challenge students to take on a variety of diverse perspectives.

Teacher Feature

Tanya Diaz is a science and STEAM coach. During her body systems unit with third graders, she wanted to go beyond worksheets and labeling. Instead, simulating the board game Operation, she put students in the roles of surgeons. She began by giving her students patient reports and then asked students to put the "body" back together, focusing on the key terms and functions of the four major body systems. She created simulations with real materials, such as vinegar for gastric juice and baking soda to simulate bile and pancreas enzymes. This is a great example of close

> reading and kinesthetic learning, using the formal lens with students in an engaging, unique role. You can find out more about Tanya and this activity on her Instagram @giftedteacher305.

HISTORY LENS

A history lens is used when we draw on historical knowledge to discover something about our content. This use of a history lens comes from structuralism, a literary theory that studies the structure of literature to discover patterns and principles. Traditionally, a history lens is tied to literature; however, there are two ways it connects to your content:

1. The first way we can use a history lens is the most common. We simply talk about the historical basis for our content. Easy! This one applies to any class. For example, in library class, you may teach students about the history of books and recordkeeping.
2. The second way is more closely tied to reading, but you don't have to be an ELA teacher to use this lens. Any content area class that involves a book gives an opportunity to discover the history and culture of the time it was written in or written about. This shows us how books and informational texts reveal cultural, political, and historical patterns, themes, attitudes, and biases of the time. In a middle school Spanish class, for example, you may explore the historical and cultural connections to the Great Depression and Mexican farm labor camps in *Esperanza Rising* by Pam Muñoz Ryan.

Why It Matters

Whether you're a history teacher or not, all teachers are students of history. History is interwoven with all subjects. Of course, you'll find connections to social history with just about any topic. It's also important to consider your own history and your students' histories when deciding how you teach what you teach.

> **Teacher Feature** Emily Aierstok, a middle school ELA teacher, incorporates a history lens in many of her ELA units. For example, during a research unit called "The Truth about Your Clothes," Emily's students take on the role of researcher as they explore where their own clothes are made and learn about the harsh reality of garment factories and labor practices around the world. Using a history lens, she provides context with a lesson on the Triangle Shirtwaist Factory fire, one of the deadliest industrial disasters in US history. You can learn more about Emily and her resources on her Instagram @readitwriteitlearnit.

LEARNER LENS

A learner lens is all about the learner. When you ask your students, "What do you think this means?" you're validating their perspective and connection to the content. This is the learner lens. I used to call this the reader lens after reader-response theory, but I wanted to make it more about learning any content than just the meaning of a book. The primary goal of the learner lens is to validate your students' feelings and interpretations about what they read and learn.

I know you might be thinking: What happens when they get something wrong? There are a few caveats with the learner lens I want to clarify. While it's vital to give students a voice, we must also acknowledge that not all opinions are equally valuable; this is true for adults and children. In other words, it's worthwhile to give our students a way to express their views. Still, they should understand that using expression, detail, and sources can strengthen their reactions and responses.

This distinction is important because we want to empower students to make meaningful connections to the content. The key is asking the right questions or providing the right prompts to channel their voice without undermining the curriculum.

Here's what this could look like in different classrooms:

1. A science teacher assigns a nature journal, asking students to record observations and reflections about the natural world.
2. An ELA teacher facilitates a discussion about students' opinions about the end of *The Giver* by Lois Lowry.
3. A physical education teacher asks students to freewrite about their favorite unit of the year.

Why It Matters

Many of us sat quietly in our seats, waiting for our teacher to tell us exactly what a book, film, short story, personal narrative, documentary, or artwork meant. It can be empowering to ask students to consider before you guide them to meaning. The learner lens is versatile because it's all about the learner. Therefore, you can get creative in terms of how you engage students with the lens.

> **Teacher Feature** Christopher Meckes, culinary arts and high school career exploration teacher, shows us just how easy and effective it is to bring the learner lens to any classroom. He uses a family and consumer science bell ringer journal. A bell ringer journal is a student resource filled with prompts and questions to prime students for learning at the beginning of class. This journal offers students the

opportunity to reflect and connect to their own interests. Here's an example from Christopher's bell ringer journal:

- "A well displayed meal is enhanced one hundred per cent in my eyes."—Antoine Careme
- Do you believe that the appearance of a dish matters? Why or why not?

A bell ringer or beginning of the class prompt like this one is a great way to encourage student connections to the content, drive interest in the topic, and facilitate productive discussion to begin a lesson. You can find this learner lens resource on TeachersPayTeacher.com at Twins and Teaching Culinary Arts and FACS. Christopher and his wife, Arlene, who is also an educator, blog at twinsandteaching.com, and you can also find them on Instagram @twins_and_teaching.

THE SUPPORTING LENSES

The Fab Four is a great starting point to consider lesson lenses in your planning, but the magic really happens when you challenge students to "see" your content from a variety of diverse perspectives.

In this section, I'll give you six more lesson lenses to inspire your planning with perspective. While there are undoubtedly many more literary lenses I could give for ELA teachers based on literary theory, this list is meant for any subject area.

You'll notice some intersection between the Fab Four and the supporting lenses. Please use these lenses as inspiration to develop your own if you have more to add.

The end goal is to connect these lenses with student roles, so the lesson lens ideas here are simply a teacher planning strategy to get to that end. There are so many ways to "see" learning!

ARCHETYPE LENS

An archetype lens explores patterns in literature, learning, and life. Formally, an archetype is a pattern of behavior or characteristics in real people you know or characters in stories. It could be common symbols or ideas carried across generations and cultures.

I bet you could easily name a famous mentor "type." Here are a few I came up with across different pop culture genres: Splinter in the *Teenage Mutant Ninja Turtles*, M in *James Bond*, and Mickey in *Rocky*. What do they all have in common? Each is a guide to other characters in the story. I'm confident you can think of one mentor you've had who encompassed similar characteristics.

Using an archetype lens in your classroom means looking for and analyzing patterns in fiction and fact. Here are some ideas:

1. For a social studies lesson, study the patterns of migration.
2. For an art lesson, study the patterns related to famous art movements.
3. For a social-emotional learning lesson, study the patterns of procrastination.

Why It Matters

Identifying patterns in our content and the real world helps students identify connections, make predictions, and draw conclusions. When we encourage students to "see" patterns in life and learning, they can decide if they're helpful or hurtful, then act to make a change.

> **Teacher Feature**
>
> Ana Perez, a technology and teacher coach, gives us an excellent example of the archetype lens. To celebrate poetry month, her students read "We Wear the Mask" by Paul Laurence Dunbar and "Jabari Unmasked" by Nikki Grimes. Using an archetype lens to study the symbolic meaning of a mask across time and culture, students became artists to create their own papier-mâché masks and write their own Golden Shovel poems. You can learn more about Ana and this activity on her Instagram account @simply.ana.p.

ARTISTIC LENS

The artistic lens comes from aesthetic theory, a school of criticism that studies the influence of art and art movements on literature. The word *aesthetic* means "related to beauty or the appreciation of beauty." Applied to learning, the artistic lens promotes the importance of art and artistic movements.

Many elementary teachers are masters of the artistic endeavor in their classrooms, given that lower-grade curriculums often include hands-on activities. Middle school and high school teachers may have to challenge themselves to add more smart art to their classrooms. You can use art to reconceptualize a task or as a new piece of content to supplement your content area. Here are some ideas:

1. When teaching the parts of a cell in science class, analyze a watercolor painting of the cell by molecular artist David Goodsell. Then have students create their own artistic renderings of the cell.
2. In math class, conduct experiments that connect music and math. PBS Learning Media, for example, has interactive

experiments in their Chrome Music Lab for students in grades 3–12 that show the relationship between music and math.[1]
3. When studying Victorian literature in a high school English class, ask students to design a paper doll and fashion-forward outfits that represent the aesthetic movement of the time.

Why It Matters

If you've ever been told you have an eye for fashion, photography, or art or an ear for music, the artistic lens is for you. And even if you haven't, the artistic lens is still for you. Studying art can literally challenge our visual perspectives, encouraging us to see content from a new point of view.

> **Teacher Feature** Megan Forbes, introduced in chapter 3, is a middle school social studies teacher who teaches world history. The study of ancient art is a foundation in her class, and her students use an artistic lens to explore the artifacts in place of texts. You can learn about Megan and these activities on her YouTube channel Too Cool for Middle School and on Instagram @toocoolformiddleschool.

CULTURE LENS

Culture refers to the customs, achievements, and social characteristics of a particular nation, people, or social group. As we learned in part 1 of this book, identities, and therefore culture, are complex. So the culture lens relates to two activities. First, the culture lens encourages us to explore ourselves, reflecting on our own culture. Second, the culture lens means discovering, recognizing, and celebrating the cultures of others.

The culture lens closely intersects with other lenses. For example, culture and history and culture and power are closely connected. Using a culture lens in your class can relate to students' research on their ancestry, exploration into their identities, and study of different cultures.

Why It Matters

Multicultural education is at the heart of multiple perspectives in schools, and there are crossover benefits, such as increased empathy and open-mindedness.[2] Understanding, accepting, and valuing cultural differences is at the heart of an accepting society.

> **Teacher Feature** Asia Hines, a middle school math teacher, shows us a great example of how a cultural lens can be used to prep for mathematics standardized tests. She created a global adventure for her students aimed at reviewing the math standardized test in her state. Giving students a virtual map, she takes them on a virtual trip to visit and learn about different countries while they review for their standardized test. Learning about these countries and their cultures is a great example of a cultural lens, but what makes this even better is that she selected the countries based on her students' diverse backgrounds. You can find out more about Asia and this activity on her Instagram @thesassyteacher.

NATURE LENS

The nature lens is used to look to nature for answers about life and learning. It was inspired by eco-criticism, which explores the relationship between nature and humanity. To preserve the natural world, the nature lens encourages us to explore how humans represent, interact with, and affect the natural world.

This lens isn't limited to science class. Our interactions with nature can be purely pedagogical or they can be content-related. In "Inspired by Nature," chapter 18 of *Keeping the Wonder*, we provide a list of over fifteen ideas for outdoor learning (as a bonus the titles are alliterative, so they sound nice, too). My favorites are Grassy Gallery Walk and Socratic Senses. Both instructional activities, a gallery walk or a Socratic seminar, are typically indoor activities that can be moved outside to use a nature lens.

You can also look at content with an eye to nature by identifying connections between your curriculum and the natural world. Science is obvious, so let's look at other content areas:

1. Literature is riddled with references to nature.
2. Natural art is its own branch.
3. Number sequences are often found in nature, such as Fibonacci's spiral in a shell.
4. Geography studies the physical features of the earth and atmosphere.
5. Physical education relies on outdoor spaces for many activities.

Why It Matters

Nature is a source of both anguish and inspiration. It's all around us. We can't escape it, so we might as well embrace it.

> **Teacher Feature**
> Nancy Chung, a fifth-grade teacher, is a craft-tivities and DIY expert. There are engaging ideas for all lenses on her Instagram and TikTok pages. One popular activity on social media caught my eye because it so beautifully and skillfully uses the nature lens. During a lesson on writing haiku poetry, students used *National Geographic* photo pages layered with clear transparency

paper to trace beautiful drawings of wildlife. Their new nature artwork inspired their haiku poems. Students used their nature lens as an inspiration and connection to the ELA lesson. You can find tutorials for this project and much more on her Instagram and TikTok @fancynancyin5th.

POWER LENS

The power lens is a conglomeration of many different literary, social, and historical theories exploring how class, race, gender, religion, ethnicity, nationality, political beliefs, and religion affect people of the past or present. As a result, this lens is related to many different academic disciplines, such as politics, law, media studies, anthropology, art, and philosophy. The goal of the power lens is to assess who holds the power and what they do with it.

This lens can be broken up into many more lenses for each of the issues listed above. However, they all have one thing in common: they explore how power is distributed and how it affects those who do not possess it. This lens is an excellent way to dive into the complexity of power because someone might have power in one way but not in others. Therefore, it's a great tool to evaluate how power is used to help or harm.

Eric Liu's TED Talk titled "How to Understand Power"[3] provides a great access point to consider civic power as it relates to multiple classroom contexts:

1. Physical force—how physical force relates to power through the threat of violence
2. Wealth—how money can buy power

3. Control of government—how power is distributed through governmental operations
4. Social norms—how social acceptance holds power over people's actions
5. Ideas—how power is earned through shared values and can motivate people to take up a cause
6. Vocal mass—how power can be achieved through numbers

From statistics to physical education to history to literature to human behaviors, the exploration of power can be applied to any classroom context. For older students, you could ask them to consider which areas apply to different circumstances. For younger students, you may explain one area of power and ask them to apply it to a situation.

Why It Matters

The people with the power write the rules, and they do it without the knowledge of the masses. Teaching students to analyze constructs of power is, therefore, a valuable lens to consider important social, historical, and cultural contexts, as well as in their everyday lives.

> **Teacher Feature** My husband Mike is a high school history and government and politics teacher. I must give him credit for introducing me to Liu's TED Talk, so I wanted to feature how he uses the elements of power in his class. Specifically, he uses the power lens to explore current events in his AP US government and politics class. When reviewing headlines and news stories, he'll ask his students to analyze the elements of power at play: physical force, wealth, control of government, social norms, ideas, and vocal mass. They discuss which elements of power are most important or least important and why it matters.

SOCIAL-EMOTIONAL LENS

The social-emotional lens is a way to support our students' development of essential social and emotional skills and attitudes by exploring your course content. Inspired by psychoanalysis, a theory about how the mind works, this lens is influenced by the father of psychology, Sigmund Freud, and his studies on the human psyche.

Using a social-emotional lens in your class can be a great way to tap into social-emotional learning (SEL). This lens can often be tied to reading as students can learn about behaviors, decision-making, and beliefs and attitudes through fictional characters before applying this learning to their own lives. But that's only one way. Closely tied to the learner lens, the social-emotional lens encourages students to develop their social and emotional knowledge and skills.

There are some caveats to consider when planning with this lens. While there is less concern when discussing social and emotional situations and attitudes of fictitious characters, we need to be cautious about "diagnosing" another person's psychological or emotional state, especially when we're talking about challenging or triggering situations or events. There are tactful ways to discuss why someone might feel a certain way. This means the following:

1. Removing judgment and simply acknowledging someone's thoughts and feelings as best we can based on the information we have
2. Considering the complexity of a person's or character's conflicts, identifying how challenging decisions can be
3. Acknowledging that some things are out of a person or character's control
4. Linking your discussion to a learner lens to discuss how students feel about a situation

Why It Matters

The human condition is one of highs and lows, and the benefits of social and emotional learning are well-documented as a way to deal with these changes. In a meta-analysis of twelve meta-analyses on SEL (we're talking hundreds of studies), the results strongly indicated that SEL positively impacts prosocial behavior, academic achievement, and student attitudes, among other benefits.[4] Using a social-emotional lens to teach your content can have excellent outcomes. In addition, it's fascinating. Humans love exploring the intricacies of the brain.

> **Teacher Feature**
>
> Tahiya Cooper, a former third-grade teacher, current elementary guidance counselor, and an award-winning children's author, is an expert in promoting social-emotional learning through hands-on learning experiences and reading. Take her picture book *Kindness Week* as an exemplary classroom resource to do just that. The book was inspired by a kindness club she created in her Maryland school district, and her Instagram @hangingwithms.cooper includes many ways to bring the social-emotional lens to any classroom context using *Kindness Week* as an example. You'll find excellent ideas to celebrate the joy of helping others and perspective-taking. You can learn more about Tahiya at her author website hangingwithmisscooper.com.

Putting It All Together

You now have a list of ten lesson lenses to bring to the lesson planning table. The Fab Four ensures you'll always have four to fall back on, while the supporting lenses provide more opportunities to diversify your students' learning perspectives.

So far, we've been considering these lenses from the instructor's perspective. The definitions and examples provided aren't for students;

they're for you. Sure, you can explicitly teach these perspectives, but that's not what this process is about.

Your knowledge and understanding of different lenses are meant to springboard your creativity in planning learner-centered opportunities for students to *use* these lenses in your classroom. This is a great place to consider cross-curricular lenses.

Jonathan Barnes, author of *An Introduction to Cross-Curricular Learning*, explained this beautifully: "We each look on the world, its objects, patterns and experiences, with different eyes. Cross-curricular learning recognises these multiple viewpoints and seeks to build more knowledgeable, lasting and transferable understandings of the world around us."[5]

Making connections between subjects is an excellent way to use and modify the Fab Four lenses and the supporting lenses. In fact, I'm sure you can find connections between the lenses I've provided and other subjects. The key is considering your own curriculum and the needs of your students.

Can you think of any lenses you'd like to add? This could be a variation of the ones I included or something completely different. In the space below, give your lens a title, a definition, and of course, explain why it matters (in general and for your class).

Lens Title: _____

Definition: _____

Why It Matters

You've now learned different perspectives and ways they can be applied to a variety of classrooms, curriculum, and contexts. In chapter 5, you'll give them a role.

5

GIVE THEM A ROLE

Once you have your lenses, it's time to create an activity that engages students with your chosen perspective. Ask yourself, how will students use their new lens to explore the content?

One of the best ways to spark your creative thinking is to imagine ways to put your students in new roles to *use* the new lenses. This role-taking can be as simple as a set of directions, or you can develop an entire activity around student roles.

We're going to use the Fab Four as our examples to practice making the shift from the teacher's perspective to the student role.

The Fab Four Roles

For each of the Fab Four lenses, we'll pair the lens with a role. This first shift is essential to move us from perspective to role-play. Then, we'll brainstorm learner-centered activities that put the roles to use.

Biography Lens

Let's start with the biography lens since it has a rather obvious role. If you were going to put on magical glasses that helped you see through the biography lens, you would be a biographer.

Now you have a role. We've moved from theory (biography lens) to practice (biographer).

Let's imagine an activity a biographer would do. If you said "write a biography about a person," you're absolutely right! But that's not the only role you can practice with a biography lens.

After learning about the life of a figure in your curriculum, students could become the following:

1. Architects to design a symbolic memorial or statue for the person
2. Museum curators to explain an artifact about the person's life

Biographers, architects, and museum curators are three different roles that use a biography lens. Our goal is to create an activity in which students must take on the role and apply the lens to their learning in your class.

Here's an example:

BIOGRAPHY LENS		
The Action	**The Role**	**The Task**
Biographers are scholars who write about a person's life, and they share their findings in books and articles and on television and podcast interviews.	You are a biographer who is studying [a person related to your content]. During your research, you found an artifact about this person's life.	Create a letter, photograph, page from a journal, or important object related to the life of [person related to your content]. Prepare the artifact for display at the World Museum. Include a one-paragraph description of the artifact explaining what it is and how it is related to the author.

> **Teacher Notes**
>
> In this activity, students apply what they learned about an author to an active learning activity: creating an artifact related to the author. This is a great way to provide hands-on learning and give students a choice in their end product. For younger students, you can provide biographical information first and simplify the task. For older students, you may include a research requirement.

Your Turn

Now, you give it a try.

How could you use a biography lens in your classroom? What role will students take on? What activity will they do with their new role?

_____

_____

_____

_____

Formal Lens

A formal lens gives us more options since there isn't an obvious role to get us started. We could use many different roles. As a reminder, a formal lens helps students "see" the key parts of our content. With this lens, we have a great opportunity to turn what would probably be a worksheet or a lecture into a learner-centered, engaging activity. I came up with three examples below, but you can probably think of many others.

After reading about the key concepts in a chapter, students could become the following:

1. Artists to create a piece of artwork that represents the meaning of the story
2. A teacher to write an essay prompt or multiple-choice questions
3. A critic to write a book review for the class newspaper

Now, let's pick one and turn it into an activity:

FORMAL LENS		
The Action	**The Role**	**The Task**
Critics are specialists who evaluate the quality of something, and they use their specialty to review items for others.	You are a critic for the *Learning Times* who reviews topics from our class and writes critical reviews so other learners know what to expect.	Write a review of [the topic or the content covered in class]. First, give an overview of the [topic or content] in detail. Then, explain what is positive and negative about [the topic]. Finally, explain why people should learn about it.
Teacher Notes		
I wrote this very generally, but you can (and should) provide more parameters in your task section. Here's an example of what I mean for a high school English class (since this was my certification area): evaluate the characters (one paragraph), plot (one paragraph), and themes (one paragraph) by judging their quality. Consider how believable and likable the main characters are, how exciting and intriguing the plot was, and how meaningful the themes were. Instead of more parameters, you might want to simplify the task for early learners: Draw a picture of [the item you're reviewing], and underneath, write if you like or dislike [the topic].		

Your Turn

How could you use a formal lens in your classroom? What role will students take on? What activity will they do with their new role?

_____

_____

_____

History Lens

Here's another easy one for us! The obvious role here is a historian. Here are a few additional roles that use a history lens to give you some other ideas.

After studying the historical background of your content, students could become the following:

1. Panelists for a panel discussion about the topic to report their findings
2. Guests on a news report to report about a historical event
3. Illustrators to design the cover of their new historical book

HISTORY LENS		
The Action	**The Role**	**The Task**
Historians are experts in the study of history, geography, society, and culture, and they use their knowledge to teach others.	You were recently invited to be on the nightly news to discuss [a historical concept related to your content].	To prepare for your interview, with a partner, create a list of questions and answers related to [the topic]. Then, practice answering them without looking. You'll be asked some of these questions during your live interview. Who? What? Where? When? Why? How? To what extent?

Teacher Notes
This activity includes partner work and an extended opportunity to do a "newscast" in your classroom. If you want to take it up a notch, in groups, choose roles for the news anchors who will ask questions and the historians who will answer. You can even create the news desk! For older students, you can craft the questions to be more rigorous and related to your content, if necessary. For younger students, you can stick with who, what, where, when questions and give students more prompting.

Your Turn

How could you use a history lens in your classroom? What role will students take on? What activity will they do with their new role?

_____

_____

_____

_____

_____

Learner Lens

This is where you can really have some fun because it's all about the learner, which means you can channel anything your students are into!

After learning about a new topic, students could be the following:

1. Gamers to try out new content and give a personal review
2. Podcasters to record a podcast about their reflections on the content
3. Bloggers to write insights on the reading

Turning these roles into activities can be very open-ended. So much so, it might be fun to give them a choice.

LEARNER LENS		
The Action	**The Role**	**The Task**
Influencers have a special talent, skill, or interest in a topic, and they use this niche to influence the opinions of others about this topic.	You are an influencer in the [topic related to your class] niche who is loved for sharing the real scoop with your followers.	Choose a medium to share with your followers (podcast, short-form video, or writing). Then, write a personal review of [the topic].
Teacher Notes		

If you're not jazzed about exposing your younger students to influencer culture, you can go back to the critic activity from the formal lens. Instead of making it a critical review, make it a personal review.
    If you want to provide more parameters, here's how I would do it:
        Influencer posts usually start with a personal connection to [item being reviewed] (paragraph one). Then, they transition into an explanation of what they liked (paragraph two) and didn't like (paragraph three).		

Your Turn

How could you use a learner lens in your classroom? What role will students take on? What activity will they do with their new roles?

_____

_____

_____

_____

The Supporting Roles

I hope the Fab Four roles helped you see how to turn a lens into a role with an accompanying student activity. Because the Fab Four are our go-to lenses, we were able to get rather creative with our plans. But it doesn't always have to be so fancy. In this section, I want to show ways to combine our supporting lenses with standard roles to create simple yet effective supporting roles. This list of standard roles and actions can be paired with any lens.

In this section, we'll start with the lens, choose a role from the list, and then use the student-centered role-play activity to formulate your task. This is even easier than what we already practiced. Whereas with the Fab Four section we created unique roles and activities for each lens, in this section, we will streamline the process with a standard role from the list.

To start, review the list of standard roles and their associated activity.

STANDARD ROLE	ACTION
Actor/Actress	Perform a dramatic interpretation to illuminate the lens.
Artist	Create an artistic interpretation to illuminate the lens.
Author	Write something to examine the content with the lens.
Documentarian	Create a documentary to explore the content with the lens.
Journalist	Conduct a live or recorded interview to explore the content with the lens.
Marketing Agent	Sell a product related to the content with your lens.
Panelist	Answer questions about the content with the lens.
Philosopher	Prepare and facilitate a discussion to explore the content with the lens.
Podcaster	Create a recorded podcast to examine the content with the lens.
Researcher	Present your findings on a topic in your content with your lens.
Teacher	Create a class activity to teach the content with your lens.

The first point I hope you noticed is that they are all written in a general way so they can be paired with any lens. If you glance back over this list, you may notice I left out the roles of psychologist, doctor, or the like. This was intentional. Unless you're working with fictitious characters, you should not have students diagnose someone or something. Even if you are teaching fiction, it's a good idea to explain the context as fictitious and provide appropriate parameters.

Let's look at some examples to show how we can use supporting lenses with standard roles. The first two examples come from a unit created by Katie Fitzpatrick, a student teacher I had the honor of supervising during her practicum in a self-contained second-grade classroom.

She designed and taught a five-day mini-unit on Earth Day with encouragement and guidance from her cooperating teacher (the teacher whose classroom she was in) and me as her college supervisor. One of the unit's goals was to create meaningful, learner-centered roles for students to experience the content. Having supervised and observed Katie during her placement, I was extremely impressed with her creative lenses planning, and her cooperating teacher was very complimentary! The mini-unit was a great success on all accounts.

I will highlight two of her activities here, but you can find the entire Lenses Plan in the Resource Library at the end of the book.

Example 1—Power Lens Using a Marketing Agent Role
First up is the power lens. For this activity, Katie put students into the role of marketing agents from the list above. She began by teaching students about the three Rs (reduce, reuse, and recycle) and discussing the power that comes from environmental advocacy. Then, using the power lens to focus on vocal mass (aka power in numbers), students created posters to persuade others to follow the three Rs.

Example 2—Social-Emotional Lens Using an Author Role
The next example uses a simple author role to encourage reflection on their current and future social behaviors with a social-emotional lens. First, she conducted a read-aloud for *Here We Are: Notes for Living on*

Planet Earth by Oliver Jeffers. This picture book served as a mentor text for students to write and illustrate their own "notes for living on planet Earth."

Let's look at a secondary example. I created a mini-unit for a narrative poem most of you have probably read, and many of you probably teach or reference: "The Raven" by Edgar Allan Poe. The entire Lenses Plan Unit with commentary on what I did, how I did it, and why I did it will be outlined in chapter 6. In the meantime, here are two examples of how I used a standard role to engage students with a supporting lens:

Example 1—Archetype Lens Using an Artist Role

Symbols are important in "The Raven," specifically the archetypal symbol of the raven and the bust it lands on. Therefore, after researching one of two symbols (the raven and the bust of Pallas), students will take on the role of artists to create a partner symbol poster. The goal is for students to create an artistic collaboration, something that happens often in the real world. After students complete their posters, they will participate in a gallery walk to celebrate (and discuss) their art.

Example 2—Social-Emotional Lens Using a Panelist Role

For this example, students will take on the role of a panelist during a panel discussion. To use the social-emotional lens, their topics will be based on an area related to the narrator's emotional state, such as sadness or anger. To become experts on their topic, they will individually research their area so they can use the social-emotional lens to participate in a panel discussion with the teacher as moderator.

Both elementary and secondary examples demonstrate how easy it is to frame or reframe a traditional activity to create student-centered activities. The point is you can be as creative as you'd like when creating lens roles. Teachers who love creating an exciting, thematic classroom transformation may already have their unique student role in mind, for instance. Other times, the lenses will inspire you to create something new.

Either way, your students benefit from multiple-perspective-getting activities aligned to your unit objectives. It will create a situation in which students have a direct purpose linked to their role and, therefore, linked to the action of using a lens. As Katie reflected, "My biggest takeaway from planning a unit using different lenses and practicing it by giving students unique roles was that students had an opportunity to make learning their own."

In chapter 6, it's time to put all of these into practice so you can create your own Lenses Plan!

6

CREATE YOUR OWN VISION

Congratulations! You've made it to chapter 6, which means you're ready to create your own vision. In this chapter, I will take you through a simple process to apply all that you've learned in this book. You'll follow my Lenses Plan model to create (or rethink) your own unit.

I know how important it is to have a plan that is simple to follow and easy to re-create. Alas, if it can't happen practically and promptly, it's not happening. For the record, you can always come back to chapter 4 to refresh your background on the lenses or to chapter 5 to brainstorm new roles that align with your goals and appeal to your students.

You'll notice this chapter mimics what you learned in the first half of the book in terms of both order and content. Chapter 6 is designed for practical planning. Instead of headings, you'll find action steps. Each activity will guide you through the planning process, and I encourage you to complete them right here in your book.

If you're reading an e-book version, listening to the audiobook, or wanting a digital copy, you can go to RoleCallBook.com to download an editable version of the workbook. This will also make it possible for you to plan multiple units or lessons.

Once you've gone through the planning in this chapter at least once, you may be ready for the expedited version. There is a copy of the one-page Lenses Plan at the end of this book and in your digital download at RoleCallBook.com. I don't recommend using it until you've gone through the entire version below, and you can always come back to the longer form when you need the added support.

For each step, I'll provide an example from the Lenses Plan I mentioned in chapter 5. Specifically, the unit focuses on "The Raven" by Edgar Allan Poe to teach students how to connect character development to theme. Although this might not be your area of expertise, the point is to walk you through my thought process. Therefore, my think-aloud (write-aloud?) comments will be in italics. A blank copy of the template will follow my examples for each step so you can plan your next unit as you go.

At the very end of this section, you'll find the Role Call Resource Library with resources mentioned in this chapter. You'll also find a complete Lenses Plan for Katie's mini-unit on Earth Day so you can see both an elementary and secondary example.

Without further ado, our first stop on our perspective planning path is Step 1: See the Destination.

Step 1: See the Destination

The first step to streamline the perspective-planning process is setting the objective(s) for the unit. I know "objective" sounds formal, so let's continue with our tour-guide teacher analogy and think of it as our destination. In other words, where should students be by the end of the unit? Once we know the destination, we can create our Lenses Plan with pit stops and checkpoints (activities and assessments) along the way.

Destination: First, let's start with your ideal destination for students. At the end of this journey, where should students be and/or what should they be able to do?

By the end of this unit, students should be able to. . .explain how the theme of "The Raven" by Edgar Allan Poe is developed through the use of symbolism and character development.

Travel Obligations: Let's ensure you're also meeting your travel obligations before you take flight. Are there any objectives set forth by your school, state or Common Core standards, Advanced Placement, etc., that you need to address? If so, record them here.

The education standards addressed in this unit are. . .

CCSS.ELA-LITERACY.RL.9-10.2
Determine a theme or central idea of a text and analyze in detail its development over the course of the text, including how it emerges and is shaped and refined by specific details; provide an objective summary of the text.

CCSS.ELA-LITERACY.RL.9-10.3
Analyze how complex characters (e.g., those with multiple or conflicting motivations) develop over the course of a text, interact with other characters, and advance the plot or develop the theme.

The standards for this unit and the objectives go hand-in-hand.

"Pics or Didn't Happen": If you can't show a pic, the kids say you don't have proof it happened. Following the backward design model from chapter 3, identify how students will show proof they made it to their destination. What summative (final) assessment will you use to show they made it to their destination?

By the end of this unit, students will show they mastered the learning objective(s) by. . .*writing a thematic argument essay.*
    Prompt:
        In "The Raven," Edgar Allan Poe tells a story of a man who is visited by an unusual raven. Through his interactions with the raven, the reader learns that the narrator's emotional state impacts his reliability. Explain how the development of this narrator illuminates a theme of the work.

I wrote the prompt before I moved on to the next step, so I would have clarity with the task as I created learning opportunities for the students. It's a good idea to create your summative assessment before moving on.

Step 1: See the Destination

Destination: First, let's start with your ideal destination for students. At the end of this journey, where should students be and/or what should they be able to do?
By the end of this unit, students should be able to . . .

Travel Obligations: Let's ensure you're also meeting your travel obligations before you take flight. Are there any objectives set forth by your school, state or Common Core standards, Advanced Placement, etc., that you need to make sure you address? If so, record them here.
The educational standards addressed in this unit are . . .

"Pics or Didn't Happen": If you can't show a pic, the kids say you don't have proof it happened. Following the backward design model from chapter 3, identify how students will show proof they made it to their destination. What summative (final) assessment will you use to show they made it to their destination?
By the end of this unit, students will show they mastered the learning objective(s) by. . .

Step 2: Try a New Lens

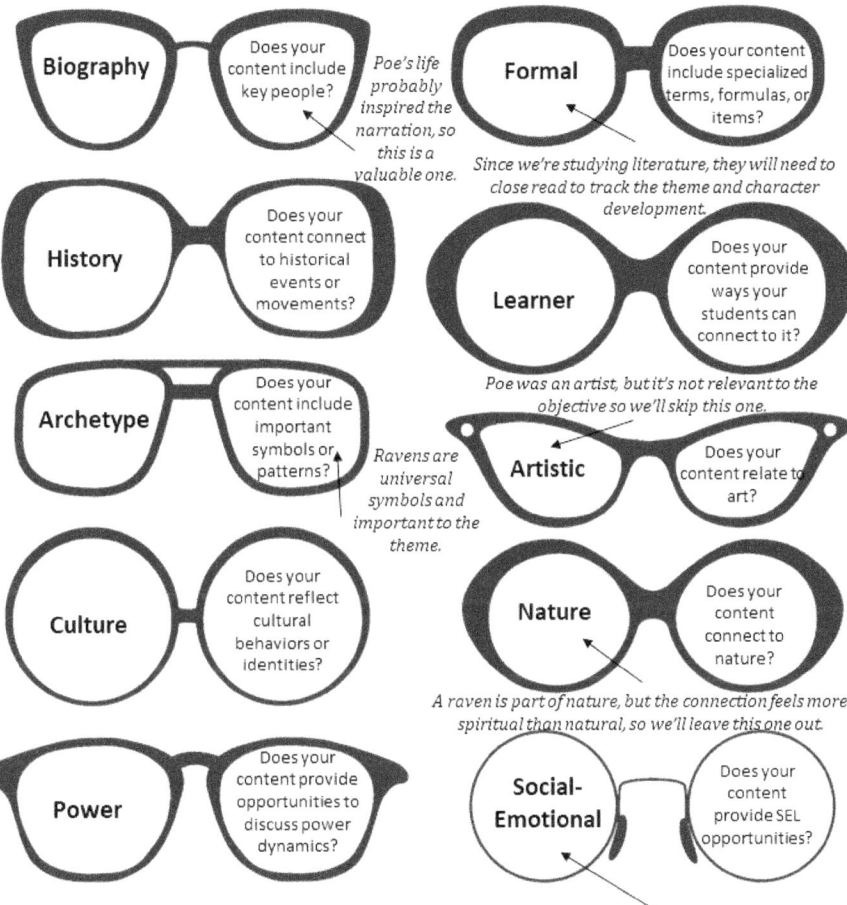

For this unit, I identified four lenses that will help students meet their objective and give me feedback toward their progress. You'll notice that I left out lenses that applied to the unit but didn't help students achieve their objective. Now, it's time for you to give it a try. Remember to connect the lens to the objective.

Step 2: Try a New Lens

Here is an overview of the all the lenses covered in chapter 4. The Fab Four start the list, and the supporting lenses finish them out. The blank lens is a space for you to add any other lenses relevant to your unit. As you review each lens, ask yourself the question. If your answer is yes, highlight the perspectives that are relevant to your unit.

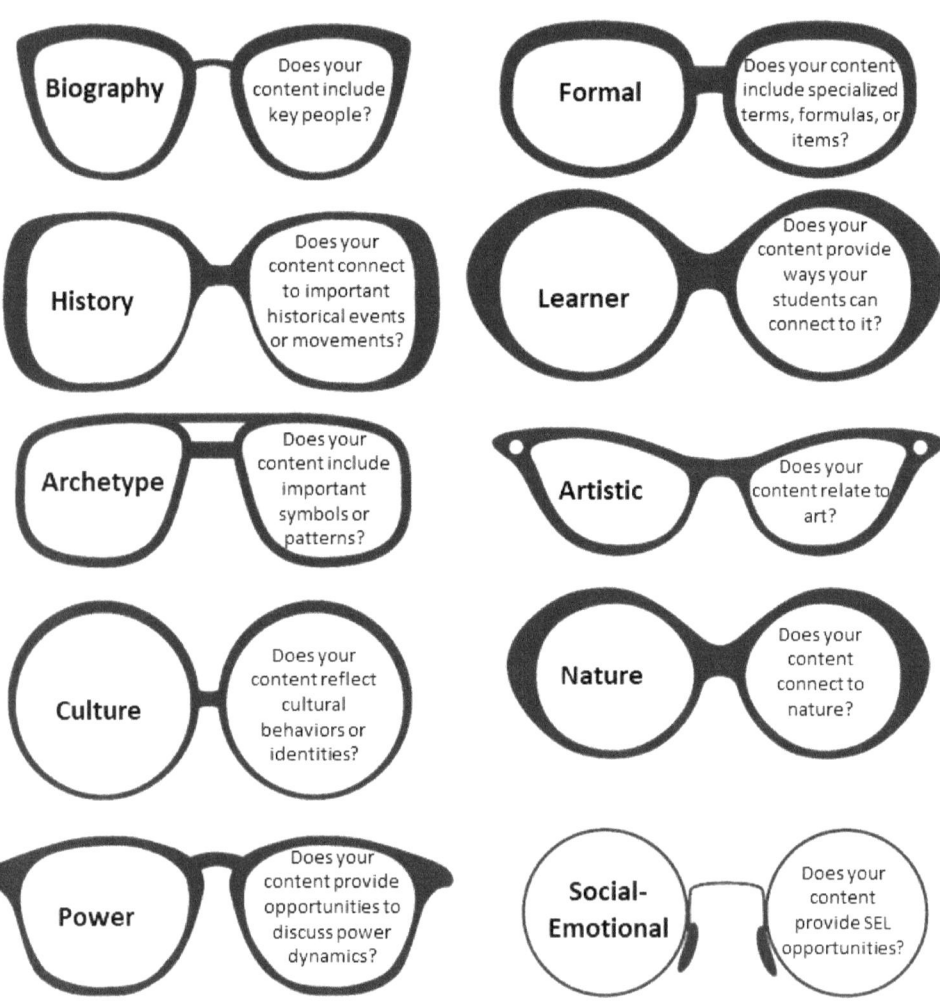

Step 3: Create Your Vision

Now that you've identified the relevant lenses for your content, you can use those lenses to create roles. Read the actions related to the lenses you choose in step 3. Then, brainstorm a specific role your students can take on to complete the action.

LENS	THE ACTION	THE ROLE
Biography	Research key people's lives and influences on the topic	*An investigator who explores Poe's life and death*
Formal	Explore the specialized terms, formulas, or items related to the topic	*A scholar who tracks the narrator's emotional response throughout the story*
History	Interpret important historical, political, or cultural events related to the topic	
Learner	Connect to the topic in a personal way	
Archetype	Examine the topic for patterns and symbols	*An artist who creates a symbolic poster*
Artistic	Analyze the artistic connections to the topic	
Culture	Identify cultural connections to the topic	

You'll notice that there is some overlap between the roles, which happens fairly often. When you apply backward design to plan your units, you'll have a learning focus that creates this overlap. It's fine either way!

I want to point out the difference between the artist lens and the artist role. While there is some overlap here, too, the lens focuses more on an artistic movement connection while the artist role involves the creation of art.

Nature	Discover the relationship between nature and the topic	
Power	Assess the dynamics of power related to the topic	
Social-Emotional	Analyze the emotional reactions to the topic	*A panelist who specializes in an area of psychology related to "The Raven"*

A panel discussion is an excellent activity to get students prepared for student-led discussions. Because the teacher has the option to be the moderator, it provides just enough structure to encourage active participation for each student. I'll include full directions in the Role Call Resource Library.

Step 3: Create Your Vision

Now that you've identified the relevant lenses for your content, you can use those lenses to create roles. Read the actions related to the lenses you choose in step 3. Then, brainstorm a specific role your students can take on to complete the action.

Lens	The Action	The Role
Biography	Research key people's lives and influences on the topic	
Formal	Explore the specialized terms, formulas, or items related to the topic	
History	Interpret important historical, political, or cultural events related to the topic	
Learner	Connect to the topic in a personal way	
Archetype	Examine the topic for patterns and symbols	
Artistic	Analyze the artistic connections to the topic	
Culture	Identify cultural connections to the topic	
Nature	Discover the relationship between nature and the topic	
Power	Assess the dynamics of power related to the topic	
Psychological	Analyze the emotional reactions to the topic	

Step 4: Plan Your Lesson Snapshot

Select three to five roles (or more!) from the last step and write them in the activity space provided. Then, define the task like we did in chapter 5. The key to streamlining the planning process is to write the task with a direct action your students will take. Therefore, I suggest starting with an action verb, like our practice with the Fab Four.

The Role	The Task
An investigator who researches Poe's life and death and the connection to "The Raven"	For this activity, students will complete research on Poe's life and death with a profile handout. As an investigator, they will determine the best theory for Poe's death, and they will share it with the class.
I wanted to include this activity to show that it doesn't have to be fancy to be effective. Poe's life and death are so fascinating that it doesn't take much to get students engaged. This activity is facilitated through a simple worksheet, but the class discussion will be lively and meaningful!	
An investigator who tracks the narrator's emotional response throughout the story	As a class, students will create a scale for emotional reactions and add those to the y-axis. Then, as they read, they will add important plot points to the bottom x-axis. During a second close read, they will plot the narrator's emotions on the scale, providing evidence from the text at each plot point. At the end of the activity, the class will share their graphs and look for similarities and common themes.
This activity will encourage students to close read with a connection to the psychological lens. It not only supports understanding the plot, but also has them focus on the objectives of the unit.	
An artist who creates a symbolic rendering of "The Raven"	After researching one of two symbols (the raven and the bust of Pallas), students will work with a partner to create a symbol poster.

A panelist who specializes in an area of psychology related to "The Raven"	For this culminating lens activity, students will specialize in one of four areas, each related to a theme and the objective of the unit. They will individually research their area and then participate in a panel discussion with the teacher as moderator.

Partner posters, alternatively called collaborative posters, are perfect for this lens because the archetype of the raven and the pairing with the symbol of the bust of Pallas have individual meaning and they provide contrast to each other. After students work with their partners, we'll do a gallery walk to look for common insights.

What I love about panel discussions is they can be modified to fit the needs of your students. You can make it a true student-led discussion and have a student be the moderator, or you can be the moderator to give more structure and focus to the activity. I also like that students are on the panel with only four to five other students at a time, giving them plenty of opportunities to contribute. The audience (the rest of the class when they're not on the panel) can still be involved. They can participate in a back-channel chat to ask questions, or you can have them write in questions for the panel.

Step 4: Plan Your Lesson Snapshot

Select three to five roles from the last step and write them in the activity space provided. Then, define the task like we did in chapter 5. The key to streamlining the planning process is to write the task with a direct action your students will take. Therefore, I suggest starting with an action verb, like our practice with the Fab Four.

The Role	The Task

Step 5: Create a Pacing Overview

It's time to get organized. Create a pacing overview to keep you organized during the unit. In the daily pacing table, add activities, assessments, notes, etc., for each day of the unit. This overview will help you decide the logical order for the activities students will complete. Will they need a day to read or research before a specific lens? If so, build that into your Lenses Plan.

Day 1	Day 2	Day 3	Day 4	Day 5
Formal Lens	Formal Lens	Formal Lens	Biography Lens	Biography Lens and Social-Emotional Lens
Read an article about the stages of grief.	Read "The Raven" as a class and instruct students to map the plot points.	Assign small groups and instruct students to share their Emotion Tracking Close Reads, looking for common themes.	Show a mini-bio on Poe and discuss parts related to "The Raven."	Facilitate the Death Theories discussion as a class.
Explain the Emotion Tracking Close Read activity.	Review the plot points together. Instruct students to reread "The Raven" and complete the Emotion Tracking Close Read.	Discuss as a class.	Explain the Poe Profile activity and instruct students to research and complete it.	Explain the Panel Discussion activity and instruct students to prepare for their role.

This pacing guide is based on 45-minute class periods.

It shows my role in engineering student success. Therefore, all the action verbs are related to my tasks.

This mini-unit is only ten days, but you can see how the same process would work for shorter or longer units.

Day 6	Day 7	Day 8	Day 9	Day 10
SOCIAL-EMOTIONAL LENS Facilitate the panel discussion.	ARCHETYPE LENS Explain the Partner Poster activity and instruct students to complete their roles individually and with their partners.	ARCHETYPE LENS Display the posters around the room and facilitate a gallery walk to look for common themes. Discuss as a class.	ASSESSMENT Facilitate the essay assignment.	ASSESSMENT Facilitate the essay assignment.

Step 5: Create a Pacing Overview

Day 1	Day 2	Day 3	Day 4	Day 5

Day 6	Day 7	Day 8	Day 9	Day 10

Day 11	Day 12	Day 13	Day 14	Day 15

Day 16	Day 17	Day 18	Day 19	Day 20

Day 21	Day 22	Day 23	Day 24	Day 25

CONCLUSION: ADMIRE THE VIEW

Congratulations! You've made it to our final destination. Now that you've learned about the research on perspective-getting and backward designed an entire unit's worth of activities that will engage students in multiple perspective-getting, it's time to admire the view! Over the next days or weeks of this unit, you'll take your students on an active learning journey through different perspectives, preparing them to make it to their destination.

Did they make it to their destination? Go back to the "Pics or It Didn't Happen" part of step 1. Then, use this space to record, reflect, and revise. Remember, curriculum planning is a cyclic process. You can (and should) go back to step 4 each year to reflect on your current activities and brainstorm new ones.

To conclude *Role Call*, I want to leave you with a one-page version of this process so you can see how easily it can be replicated in a shorter format. You'll find all the resources discussed earlier in the Role Call Resource Library. You can also get editable versions of all these handouts at RoleCallBook.com.

Lenses Plan for "The Raven"

Class	Unit/Topic	Grade(s)
English Language Arts	"The Raven" by Edgar Allan Poe	7–12
Standards		

The educational standards addressed in this unit are . . .
1. Determine a theme or central idea of a text and analyze in detail its development over the course of the text, including how it emerges and is shaped and refined by specific details; provide an objective summary of the text.
2. Analyze how complex characters (e.g., those with multiple or conflicting motivations) develop over the course of a text, interact with other characters, and advance the plot or develop the theme.

Learning Objective

By the end of this unit, students should be able to. . .
explain how the theme of "The Raven" by Edgar Allan Poe is developed through the use of symbolism and character development.

Evidence

By the end of this unit, students will show they mastered the learning objective(s) by. . . writing a thematic argument essay.

Prompt:
In "The Raven," Edgar Allan Poe tells a story of a man who is visited by an unusual raven. Through his interactions with the raven, the reader learns that the narrator's emotional state impacts his reliability. Explain how the development of the narrator illuminates a theme of the work.

Lens	The Action	The Role	The Task
Biography	Research key people's lives and influences on the topic	An investigator	*For this activity, students will complete research on Poe's life and death with a profile handout.*
Formal	Explore the specialized terms, formulas, or items related to the topic	A scholar	*Students will track the narrator's emotional responses throughout the story.*
History	Interpret important historical, political, or cultural events related to the topic		
Learner	Connect to the topic in a personal way		
Archetype	Examine the topic for patterns and symbols	An artist	*After researching one of two symbols (the raven and the bust of Pallas), students will work with a partner to create a symbol poster.*
Artistic	Analyze the artistic connections to the topic		
Culture	Identify cultural connections to the topic		
Nature	Discover the relationship between nature and the topic		
Power	Assess the dynamics of power related to the topic		
Social-Emotional	Analyze the social and emotional connections to the topic	Panelist	*Students will individually research their area and then participate in a panel discussion with the teacher as moderator.*

Role Call Resource Library

As promised, the Role Call Resource Library has example one-page Lenses Plans for the two units discussed in chapter 5: my secondary mini-unit on "The Raven" and Katie's elementary mini-unit on Earth Day.

If you are an English teacher looking for resources specific to literary lenses versus lesson lenses, you can find my bestselling Literary Lenses Workbook at RoleCallBook.com. It includes twelve literary lenses with definitions and activities more specific to teaching literature. As you saw with my example mini-unit for "The Raven," lesson lenses work just as well!

Speaking of the Poe resources, I also added the handouts referenced in my "The Raven" mini-unit so you can see how I easily turned them into activities for students. I purchased the line clip art with a commercial license from Finntastic Visuals, and I added text boxes with explicit instructions for each activity. This isn't necessary for every activity, but it helps me stay organized and collect formative feedback as I make my way through the pacing guide.

Finally, I included more formal directions for the panel discussion and gallery walk. If you liked these activities, *Keeping the Wonder: An Educators' Guide to Magical, Engaging, and Joyful Learning* is a perfect companion to *Role Call*. *Keeping the Wonder* is filled with high-engagement, learner-centered activities that pair beautifully with the Role Call method. *Role Call* gives you the framework, and *Keeping the Wonder* gives you the strategies.

Class	Unit/Topic	Grade(s)

Standards

The educational standards addressed in this unit are . . .

Learning Objective

By the end of this unit, students should be able to. . .

Evidence

By the end of this unit, students will show they mastered the learning objective(s) by. . .

Lens	The Action	The Role	The Task
Biography	Research key people's lives and influences on the topic		
Formal	Explore the specialized terms, formulas, or items related to the topic		
History	Interpret important historical, political, or cultural events related to the topic		
Learner	Connect to the topic in a personal way		
Archetype	Examine the topic for patterns and symbols		
Artistic	Analyze the artistic connections to the topic		
Culture	Identify cultural connections to the topic		
Nature	Discover the relationship between nature and the topic		
Power	Assess the dynamics of power related to the topic		
Social-Emotional	Analyze the social and emotional connections to the topic		

POE PROFILE

Born:

Died:

Life influences related to "The Raven":

❖

❖

❖

❖

Death
Theory:

Support:

EDGAR ALLAN POE

EMOTION TRACKING CLOSE READ

As a class, you will create a scale for emotional reactions from neutral at zero to the most extreme at the fifth mark and add those to the y-axis. Then, as you read, add important plot points to the bottom axis that demonstrate important emotional shifts. During a second close read, plot the narrator's emotions on the scale providing evidence from the text at each plot point. At the end of the activity, you will share your graph with the class and look for similarities and common themes.

- Acceptance
- Depression
- Bargaining
- Anger
- Denial

PANEL DISCUSSION

For this activity, you will be an expert panelist who specializes in one theme from "The Raven." After researching your topic, you will participate in a panel discussion. Groups of four will be brought up to the front of the room to discuss the four panel questions (below). You should be prepared to answer the questions using your expertise. When you're not on the panel, you will be an audience member who takes notes on the insights from the discussion.

Grief Expert

Your role is to explain how memory and loss affect a grieving individual. Then, judge how the narrator is dealing with grief through memory.

Hope Expert

Your role is to provide strategies for people dealing with hopelessness. Explain the advice you would give someone in the narrator's position.

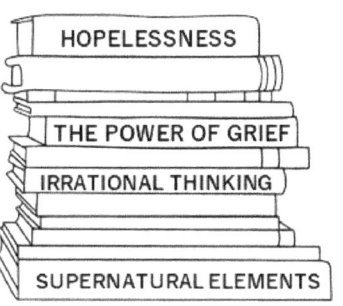

Rationality/Irrationality Expert

Your role is to explain how we determine rational behavior from irrational behavior. Then, apply your expertise to the narrator's behavior.

Supernatural Expert

Your role is to analyze the presence of the raven in the poem and determine if there was a supernatural influence. Provide your expertise by explaining your stance.

Panel Discussion Questions

1) Is the raven really there? Explain.

2) Is the narrator's behavior normal considering his situation? Explain.

3) Is the narrator trustworthy? Explain.

4) What do you think will happen to the narrator following this poem? Explain.

THE RAVEN

Research the symbolic representation of a raven and record your findings on your paper. Then, with your partner, create a partner poster. Finally, compare your notes and together, explain how the raven and the bust of Pallas establish a theme.

PARTNER RESPONSE

PARTNER RESPONSE

Research the symbolic representation of the bust of Pallas and record your findings on your paper. Then, with your partner, create a partner poster. Finally, compare your notes and together, explain how the raven and the bust of Pallas establish a theme.

THE BUST OF PALLAS

Panel Discussion Directions

Here's what I love about it:

1. All students are engaged because they all get a chance to be on the panel. When they're in the audience, they participate in a digital or print version of a virtual chat, just like a real audience does. The panel has only four or five members, so each student gets plenty of opportunities to participate; once they've contributed to the discussion several times (you can determine the number), the students rotate, so new panel members come in and out.
2. My role as the teacher can be as big or as little as I want. I can be the moderator of the discussion, or I can hand that role over to a student.
3. The discussion is guided by the moderator, so the nature of the discussion is targeted, on level for the grade/ability level, and content focused.
4. It is so easy to set up.

Step 1:
Decide on the number of students you want on the panel. Four or five students is a good number for my class. Fewer than four students makes it hard to generate discussion; more than five students makes it challenging to give everyone an equal turn.

Step 2:
Compile a list of topics for discussion. I like to use topics that focus on a central theme or concept for the work as a whole, like I did for "The Raven." I give each student a topic or two and instruct them to become an expert on those topics. I encourage them to take notes with points they might want to bring up during the discussion.

Step 3:

To prepare for your end as the teacher/moderator, print the example questions included and/or create your own. I use "cue cards" to help keep me organized. After practice, you may decide to have a student moderate the discussion.

Step 4:

On the day of the panel discussion, put together a group of four or five desks for your panel and another desk facing the panel for the moderator. The "audience" should be seated in front of the panel.

Step 5:

Assign the audience a silent discussion. Either they can work in pairs to comment on the panel discussion by passing a piece of paper back and forth, or you can create a back-channel chat for students if they have access to the internet. Once a group has concluded their discussion, bring in the next group. Continue this process until each student has had a chance to participate on the panel.

Gallery Walk Directions

Here's what I love about it:

1. A gallery walk isn't as structured as learning stations or centers, so they're easier to set up, but they have a similar effect.
2. I love kinesthetic learning! This activity gets students up and moving.
3. This activity helps students focus on the bigger picture by looking for themes, similarities, and differences.
4. A gallery walk is entirely student centered, but afterward, we can have a class discussion so I can guide them to deeper analysis and understanding.

Step 1:
Choose artifacts to display around the room. In my "The Raven" example, the artifacts were students' partner posters. However, you can choose any type of artifact that supports your content. I've used student work, articles, and artwork in the past.

Step 2:
Display the artwork around the room. This is as simple as using magnets, tape, thumbtacks, or glue.

Step 3:
Give students time to explore the artifacts just as they would at an art gallery. I like to brief beforehand like a tour guide would (get it?). This helps give them some focus for their browsing.

Step 4:
After the gallery walk, debrief. Ask students what they noticed. What did they find interesting, similar, different, odd, or surprising?

Lenses Plan for Earth Day Mini-Unit
by Katie Fitzpatrick

Class	Unit/Topic	Grade(s)
Self-contained	Earth Day	2nd grade

Standards

The educational standards addressed in this unit are . . .
- Standard CC.1.5.2.B—Recount or describe key ideas or details from a text read aloud or information presented orally or through other media.
- Standard CC.1.5.2.F—Add drawings or other visual displays to presentations when appropriate to clarify ideas, thoughts, and feelings.
- Standard 3.2.2.A4—Experiment and explain what happens when two or more substances are combined (e.g. mixing, dissolving, and separated (e.g. filtering, evaporation).
- Standard 7.1.2.D—Describe regions in geographic reference using physical features.
- Standard 7.2.2.A—Identify the physical characteristics of places.

Learning Objective

By the end of this unit, students should be able to. . .
explain how the ecosystem and human behaviors are interconnected.

Evidence

By the end of this unit, students will show they mastered the learning objective(s) by. . . writing and illustrating a grade-appropriate essay based on a writing prompt.

Writing Prompt: If you could give a baby advice on how to live on Earth, what would you say?

Lens	The Action	The Role	The Task
Biography	Research key people's lives and influences on the topic		
Formal	Explore the specialized terms, formulas, or items related to the topic	*A biologist*	*After learning about carnivores and herbivores, students will categorize organisms based on their place in an ecosystem.*
History	Interpret important historical, political, or cultural events related to the topic		
Learner	Connect to the topic in a personal way	*An artist*	*Students will create drawings of each ecosystem, highlighting the characteristics that stand out to them to determine which ecosystem is their favorite.*
Archetype	Examine the topic for patterns and symbols		
Artistic	Analyze the artistic connections to the topic or content		
Culture	Identify cultural connections to the topic		

Nature	Discover the relationship between nature and the topic	An environmental scientist	*During a pollution lab, students will apply what they learned about pollution to solve an oil spill. At the end of the lab, the instructor will demonstrate what dish soap does to the oil, and then, students will discuss their roles in being a part of the solution.*
Power	Assess the dynamics of power related to the topic	A marketing agent	*After learning about the three Rs (reduce, reuse, and recycle), students will create a poster to persuade others to recycle.*
Social-Emotional	Analyze the social and emotional connections to the topic	An author	*After participating in a read-aloud for "Here We Are: Notes for Living on Planet Earth" by Oliver Jeffers, students will reflect on their behaviors and roles for being responsible community members by completing their writing and illustration prompts.*

ABOUT THE AUTHOR

Jenna Copper is an assistant professor of education at Slippery Rock University. Formerly, she was a high school English teacher for thirteen years. She also served as English department chair and a district-level technology coach for six years. She earned her PhD in instructional management and leadership from Robert Morris University in 2013, a Higher Education Teaching Certificate from Harvard University in 2020, and a Google Educator Trainer Certificate in 2018. In 2024, she earned her K–12 Reading Specialist Certification.

Starting with her dissertation study in 2013, she has researched literary theory and multiple perspectives learning applications in education to expand perspective-taking and encourage creative teaching methods. This research passion has led her to publish research related to global learning and cross-cultural communication. In addition, she has explored ways in which information and communication technology can encourage students to gain new perspectives and build empathy.

In 2021, she coauthored the bestselling book *Keeping the Wonder: An Educator's Guide to Magical, Engaging, and Joyful Learning*. She is a lead presenter for the Keeping the Wonder Workshop, which promotes creative and innovative instructional methods. Teachers from all over the United States have attended Keeping the Wonder "pop-up" professional development workshops. You can find more about Keeping the Wonder at KeepingtheWonder.com.

In addition to the Keeping the Wonder Workshop, Jenna also presents at conferences, school districts, and workshops. To book speaking engagements or professional development training, go to jennacopper.com.

You can find out more about her research and teaching by following her on Instagram and TikTok @drjennacopper.

ACKNOWLEDGMENTS

To my husband Mike, thank you for encouraging me to write this book and, of course, for giving me so many ideas and book recommendations that helped me write this book. Truly, so much of this book was inspired by you. I love you!

To my team at DBC (especially Dave, Tara, and Lindsey), thank you for believing in me and being the absolute best publishing and editing team out there!

To my mom, thank you for helping me with the tough content editing for this book and for being my biggest cheerleader. Every time I felt discouraged, you gave me the encouragement I needed to get back to it. You're the best, Mom!

To Gigi, Camilla, and Michael, thank you for always making me smile and being so helpful whenever I need a student sample! I love you to the moon and back!

To my dad, thank you for always making me feel like I can do anything. I'm so thankful you're my dad!

To Chynell, thank you for your endless depths of wisdom and support.

To Ashley, Abby, and Staci, thank you for helping me keep the wonder in my classroom and at home. I am so thankful for your encouragement and support.

To my friends and family, thank you for your support, encouragement, and laughs.

To my colleagues at the Rock, thank you for being so incredibly encouraging and supportive. I am so thankful to work with such passionate, caring educators!

Finally, to all my students, past and present, thank you for your support! Your excitement and energy for teaching brings me so much joy!

ENDNOTES

Here is a list of the sources I discussed or cited throughout the book. I primarily cited peer-reviewed scholarly studies or academic books. If not, the information comes from credible websites. If you're interested in learning more about the referenced studies, books, or websites, you can find them in order of their appearance.

Introduction

1. Jenna M. Copper, "Thinking Critically about Teaching Criticism: Using Teachers' Perceptions to Evaluate the Literary Theory Implementation Model in the Secondary English Classroom" (PhD diss., Robert Morris University, 2013), ProQuest Dissertations and Theses, 195.
2. Henrike Moll and Andrew N. Meltzoff, "How Does It Look? Level 2 Perspective-Taking at 36 Months of Age," *Child Development* 82, no. 2 (2011): 661–673, https://doi.org/10.1111/j.1467-8624.2010.01571.x.

Chapter 1

1. "The Enneagram Institute," The Enneagram Institute, 2021, https://www.enneagraminstitute.com/.
2. "BuzzFeed Quizzes," BuzzFeed, 2023, https://www.buzzfeed.com/quizzes.
3. "roll, n.1," OED Online, December 2022. Oxford University Press, December 2022.
4. Jeremy Bentham, *The Panopticon Writings* (New York: Verso, 1995).
5. "UCL," The Panopticon Bentham Project. May 17, 2018, https://www.ucl.ac.uk/benthamproject.
6. Nicolás Valencia, "The Same People Who Designed Prisons Also Designed Schools," *ArchDaily*, May 19, 2020, https://www.archdaily.com/905379/the-same-people-who-designed-prisons-also-designed-schools.
7. Plato, *The Republic* (New York: Books, Inc., 1943).
8. Sean McGowan, "The Most Misquoted Movie Lines of All Time," *The New Yorker*, December 5, 2020, https://www.newyorker.com/humor/daily-shouts/the-most-misquoted-movie-lines-of-all-time.

9   "What Is the 'Mandela Effect'?" Cleveland Clinic, May 31, 2022, https://health.clevelandclinic.org/mandela-effect/.

10 Jerrod Brown, Deb Huntley, Stephen Morgan, Kimberly D. Dodson, and Janina Cich, "Confabulation: A Guide for Mental Health Professionals," *International Journal of Neurology and Neurotherapeutics* 4, no. 070 (2017), https://doi.org/10.23937/2378-3001/1410070.

11 Daniel Gilbert, *Stumbling on Happiness* (New York: Knopf, 2006).

12 Yuval Noah Harari, *Sapiens: A Brief History of Humankind* (New York: Harper, 2015).

13 Sam McKenzie and Howard Eichenbaum, "Consolidation and Reconsolidation: Two Lives of Memories?" *Neuron* 71, no. 2 (2011): 224–233.

14 L. Hermann, "Eine Erscheinung simultanen Contrastes," *Pflügers Archiv für die gesamte Physiologie* 3 (1870): 13–15, https://doi.org/10.1007/BF01855743.

15 Joseph Jastrow, "The Mind's Eye," *Popular Science Monthly* 54 (1899): 299–312.

16 Axel Kohler, Leila Haddad, Wolf Singer, and Lars Muckli, "Deciding What to See: The Role of Intention and Attention in the Perception of Apparent Motion," *Vision Research* 48, no. 8 (2008): 1096–1106, https://doi.org/10.1016/j.visres.2007.11.020.

17 Ralph Waldo Emerson, *The Complete Works of Ralph Waldo Emerson*, Current Opinion Edition (New York: Wm. H. Wise, 1926).

18 "Implicit Bias," Perception Institute, May 17, 2017, https://perception.org/research/implicit-bias/.

19 Patricia G. Devine, Patrick S. Forscher, Anthony J. Austin, and William T. Cox, "Long-Term Reduction in Implicit Race Bias: A Prejudice Habit-Breaking Intervention," *Journal of Experimental Social Psychology* 48, no. 6 (November 2012): 1267–1278, https://doi.org/10.1016/j.jesp.2012.06.003.

20 "Project Implicit," Project Implicit IAT, 2013, https://www.projectimplicit.net.

Chapter 2

1   Yuval Noah Harari, *Sapiens: A Brief History of Humankind* (New York: Harper, 2015).

2   Leon Festinger, "A Theory of Social Comparison Processes," *Human Relations* 7, no. 2 (1954): 117–140, https://doi.org/10.1177/001872675400700202.

3   David Schmuck, Katharina Karsay, Julia Matthes, and Aleksandar Stevic, "Looking Up and Feeling Down: The Influence of Mobile Social Networking

Site Use on Upward Social Comparison, Self-Esteem, and Well-being of Adult Smartphone Users," *Telematics and Informatics* 42 (2019): 101240, https://doi.org/10.1016/j.tele.2019.101240.

4 Jenna M. Copper, "Using ICT to Establish and Facilitate Global Connections in K–12 Education," in *The Roles of Technology and Globalization in Educational Transformation*, eds. Blessing Adeoye and Gladys Arome (IGI Global, 2020), 206–220, https://doi.org/10.4018/978-1-5225-9746-9.ch016.

5 Bibb Latane and John M. Darley, "Group Inhibition of Bystander Intervention in Emergencies," *Journal of Personality and Social Psychology* 10, no. 3 (1968): 215, https://doi.org/10.1037/h0026570.

6 Solomon E. Asch, "Studies of Independence and Conformity: I. A Minority of One Against a Unanimous Majority," *Psychological Monographs: General and Applied* 70, no. 9 (1956): 1–70, https://doi.org/10.1037/h0093718.

7 Wendy Patrick, "Power Role Play: Dressing for Success Makes You Successful," *Psychology Today*, 2017, https://www.psychologytoday.com/us/blog/why-bad-looks-good/201709/power-role-play-dressing-for-success-makes-you-successful.

8 Robert Waldinger and Marc Schulz, *The Good Life: Lessons from the World's Longest Scientific Study of Happiness* (New York: Simon & Schuster, 2023).

9 Richard M. Ryan and Edward L. Deci, "Autonomy Is No Illusion: Self-Determination Theory and the Empirical Study of Authenticity, Awareness, and Will," in *Handbook of Experimental Existential Psychology*, ed. by Jeff Greenberg, Sander L. Koole, and Tom Pyszcynski (New York: Guilford Press, 2004), 449–479.

10 William S. Ryan and Richard M. Ryan, "Toward a Social Psychology of Authenticity: Exploring Within-Person Variation in Autonomy, Congruence, and Genuineness Using Self-Determination Theory," *Review of General Psychology* 23, no. 1 (2019): 99–112, https://doi.org/10.1037/gpr0000162.

11 Michael H. Kernis and Brian M. Goldman, "A Multicomponent Conceptualization of Authenticity: Theory and Research," in *Advances in Experimental Social Psychology*, Vol. 38, 283–357. Elsevier Academic Press, 2006, https://doi.org/10.1016/S0065-2601(06)38006-9.

Chapter 3

1 Alison King, "From Sage on the Stage to Guide on the Side," *College Teaching* 41, no. 1 (1993): 30–35, https://www.jstor.org/stable/27558571.

2   Scott Freeman et al., "Active Learning Increases Student Performance in Science, Engineering, and Mathematics," *Psychological and Cognitive Sciences* 111, no. 23 (2014): 8410–8415, https://doi.org/10.1073/pnas.1319030111.

3   Paulo Freire, *Pedagogy of the Oppressed* (New York: Seabury Press, 1970).

4   E. L. McWilliam, "Teaching for Creativity: From Sage to Guide to Meddler," *Asia Pacific Journal of Education* 29, no. 3 (2009): 281–293.

5   Jenna Copper, Ashley Bible, Abby Gross, and Staci Lamb, *Keeping the Wonder: An Educator's Guide to Magical, Engaging, and Joyful Learning* (San Diego: Dave Burgess, Inc., 2021).

6   Yehuda Baruch, "Role-Play Teaching: Acting in the Classroom," *Management Learning* 37, no. 1 (2006): 43–61.

7   Michelle Loucadoux, "The Step-By-Step Guide to Reverse Engineering Your 2021 Goals," *Medium*, December 30, 2020, https://michelleloucadoux.medium.com/the-step-by-step-guide-to-reverse-engineering-your-2021-goals-8bf79a77d71.

8   Grant Wiggins and Jay McTighe, *Understanding by Design* (2nd ed.) (Alexandria, VA: ASCD, 2005).

9   Linda Button, "Backward Design Process as a Curriculum Development Model," *Curriculum Essentials: A Journey*, 2021.

10 Jean Piaget and Barbel Inhelder, *The Child's Conception of Space* (London: Routledge & Kegan Paul, 1956).

11 Steffan Surdek, "Why Understanding Other Perspectives Is a Key Leadership Skill," *Forbes*, October 12, 2022, https://www.forbes.com/sites/forbescoachescouncil/2016/11/17/why-understanding-other-perspectives-is-a-key-leadership-skill/?sh=482bd89e6d20.

12 Sherrie Campbell, "Understanding the Other Person's Perspective Will Radically Increase Your Success," *Entrepreneur*, May 12, 2016, https://www.entrepreneur.com/leadership/understanding-the-other-persons-perspective-will-radically/275543.

13 *Education Week*, "Why We Must Teach Perspective-Taking When Developing Empathy," 2019. Retrieved from https://www.edweek.org/leadership/opinion-why-we-must-teach-perspective-taking-when-developing-empathy/2019/04.

14 James Southworth, "Bridging Critical Thinking and Transformative Learning: The Role of Perspective-Taking," *Theory and Research in Education* 20, no. 1 (2022): 44–63, https://doi.org/10.1177/14778785221090853.

15 Adam Galinsky and Gordon Moskowitz, "Perspective-Taking: Decreasing Stereotype Expression, Stereotype Accessibility, and In-Group Favoritism," *Journal of Personality and Social Psychology* 78, no. 4 (2000): 708–724.

16 Andrew Todd, Galen Bodenhausen, Jennifer Richeson, and Adam Galinsky, "Perspective Taking Combats Automatic Expressions of Racial Bias," *Journal of Personality and Social Psychology* 100, no. 6 (2011): 1027–1042.

17 William H. B. McAuliffe, Evan C. Carter, Juliana Berhane, Alexander Snihur, and Michael E. McCullough, "Is Empathy the Default Response to Suffering? A Meta-Analytic Evaluation of Perspective-Taking's Effect on Empathic Concern," March 5, 2019, https://doi.org/10.1177/1088868319887599.

18 C. Daniel Batson, Bruce Duncan, Paula Ackerman, Terese Buckley, and Kimberly Birch, "Empathic Emotion: A Source of Altruistic Motivation," *Journal of Personality and Social Psychology* 40 (1981): 290-302, https://doi.org/10.1037/0022-3514.40.2.290.

19 C. Daniel Batson, Shannon Early, and Giovanni Salvarani, "Perspective Taking: Imagining How Another Feels Versus Imagining How You Would Feel," *Personality and Social Psychology Bulletin* 23, no. 7 (1997): 751–758, https://doi.org/10.1177/0146167297237008.

20 Tal Eyal, Mary Steffel, and Nicholas Epley, "Perspective Mistaking: Accurately Understanding the Mind of Another Requires Getting Perspective, Not Taking Perspective," *Journal of Personality and Social Psychology* 114 (2018): 547–571, https://doi.org/10.1037/pspa0000115.

21 Debby Damen, Monique M. Pollmann, and Terri-Louise Grassow, "The Benefits and Obstacles to Perspective Getting," *Frontiers in Communication* 6 (2021), https://doi.org/10.3389/fcomm.2021.611187.

22 Sandra W. Russ and Claire E. Wallace, "Pretend Play and Creative Processes," *American Journal of Play* 6, no. 1 (2013): 136–148, https://www.proquest.com/scholarly-journals/pretend-play-creative-processes/docview/1509085677/se-2.

23 Angeline Lillard, et al., "The Impact of Pretend Play on Children's Development: A Review of the Evidence," *Psychological Bulletin* 139, no. 1 (2013): 1–34, https://doi.org/10.1037/a0029321.

24 Arpit Bawa, "Role-Play," in *The Students' Guide to Learning Design and Research*, ed. R. Kimmons and S. Caskurlu. EdTech Books, https://edtechbooks.org/studentguide/roleplay.

25 Gary C. B. Winardy and Eva Septiana, "Role, Play, and Games: Comparison Between Role-Playing Games and Role-Play in Education," *Social Sciences & Humanities Open* 8, no. 1 (2023).

26 "Where on Google Earth is Carmen Sandiego: The Crown Jewels of Caper." 2023. Google Earth. https://experiments.withgoogle.com/where-on-earth.

27 Krysia M. Yardley-Matwiejczuk, *Role Play: Theory and Practice* (London: Sage Publications, 1997).

28 Rachel Stevens, "Role-Play and Student Engagement: Reflections from the Classroom," *Teaching in Higher Education* 20, no. 5 (2015): 481–492, https://doi.org/10.1080/13562517.2015.1020778.

29 Adam Blatner, "Role Playing in Education," *Disponibile all'indirizzo*. 2009, http://www.blatner.com/adam/pdntbk/rlplayedu.htm.

30 The Zinn Education Project, "'I Saw Eyes Begin to Widen': Joys, Pitfalls, and Dilemmas in Using Role Play in the Classroom," 2002, https://rethinkingschools.org/articles/i-saw-eyes-begin-to-widen/.

31 M. D. Forbes, "Engaging without the Gimmicks: Rethinking 3 Common Social Studies Teaching Strategies." Brave History Conference [virtual], 2023.

32 Azizah C. Iluore, "'Take These Nametags Off!': Disrupting Poorly Designed Classroom Role Play," *Rethinking Schools* 36 no. 2 (2022), https://rethinkingschools.org/articles/take-these-nametags-off/.

33 Deborah Appleman, *Critical Encounters in High School English: Teaching Literary Theory to Adolescents* (New York: Teachers College Press, 2009).

34 Rudine Sims Bishop, "Mirrors, Windows, and Sliding Glass Doors," *Perspectives* 1, no. 3 (1990): ix–xi.

35 Robert Scholes, *Textual Power: Literary Theory and the Teaching of English* (New Haven: Yale University Press, 1985).

36 Lisa Schade, "Demystifying the Text: Literary Criticism in the High School Classroom," *English Journal* 85, no. 3 (1996): 26–31, https://doi.org/10.2307/820099.

37 J. Willinsky, "Teaching Literature Is Teaching in Theory," *Theory Into Practice* 37, no. 3 (1998): 244-250.

38 Catherine P. Sagan, "Sing a New Song: A Fresh Look at Literary Criticism," *English Journal* 92, no. 6 (2003): 40.

39 Joanne M. Golden and Donna Canan, "'Mirror, Mirror on the Wall': Readers' Reflections on Literature through Literary Theories," *English Journal* 93, no. 5 (2004): 42–46, https://doi.org/10.2307/4128934.

40 Melissa Troise, "Approaches to Reading with Multiple Lenses of Interpretation," *English Journal* 96, no. 5 (2007): 85–90.

41 Joyce H. Burstein and Lisa Hutton, "Planning and Teaching with Multiple Perspectives," *Social Studies and the Young Learner* 18, no. 1 (2005): 15–17.

42 Mary A. Christenson, "Teaching Multiple Perspectives on Environmental Issues in Elementary Classrooms: A Story of Teacher Inquiry," *The Journal of Environmental Education* 35, no. 4 (2004): 3–16, https://doi.org/10.3200/JOEE.35.4.3-16.

43 Charlene Cornwall, "The 'Other Side' of the Story: Designing Multiple Perspective Inquiries," National Council for the Social Studies 2018 Annual Conference, Chicago, IL, United States, 2018, https://www.socialstudies.org/sites/default/files/multiple_perspectives_ncss_presentation_1.pdf.

44 Science Media Group at the Harvard-Smithsonian Center for Astrophysics, Brian Mind et al., "Perspective Shifting in Math," [video]. *Annenberg Learner*, 2012, https://www.learner.org/series/neuroscience-in-the-classroom/implications-for-schools/perspective-shifting-in-math/.

Chapter 4

1 "Music and Math," PBS LearningMedia, 2023, https://wqed.pbslearningmedia.org/subjects/the-arts/music/music-and-other-domains/music-and-math/.

2 "The Importance of Diversity and Multicultural Education Awareness in Education," Drexel University School of Education, https://drexel.edu/soe.

3 Eric Lui, "How to Understand Power," [video], TED-Ed, https://www.ted.com/talks/eric_liu_how_to_understand_power/transcript?language=en.

4 J. Durlak, J. Mahoney, and A. Boyle, "What We Know, and What We Need to Find Out about Universal, School-Based Social and Emotional Learning Programs for Children and Adolescents: A Review of Meta-Analyses and Directions for Future Research," *Psychological Bulletin* 148, no. 11/12 (2022): 765–782, https://doi.org/10.1037/bul0000383.

5 J. Barnes, "An Introduction to Cross-Curricular Learning," in *The Primary Curriculum: A Creative Approach*, ed. Patricia Driscoll, Andrew Lambirth, and Judith Roden (London: Sage Publications, 2015), 320.

MORE FROM

Dave Burgess Consulting, Inc.

Since 2012, DBCI has published books that inspire and equip educators to be their best. For more information on our titles or to purchase bulk orders for your school, district, or book study, visit DaveBurgessConsulting.com/DBCIbooks.

The *Like a PIRATE*™ Series
Teach Like a PIRATE by Dave Burgess
eXPlore Like a PIRATE by Michael Matera
Learn Like a PIRATE by Paul Solarz
Plan Like a PIRATE by Dawn M. Harris
Play Like a PIRATE by Quinn Rollins
Run Like a PIRATE by Adam Welcome
Tech Like a PIRATE by Matt Miller

The *Lead Like a PIRATE*™ Series
Lead Like a PIRATE by Shelley Burgess and Beth Houf
Balance Like a PIRATE by Jessica Cabeen, Jessica Johnson, and Sarah Johnson
Lead beyond Your Title by Nili Bartley
Lead with Appreciation by Amber Teamann and Melinda Miller
Lead with Collaboration by Allyson Apsey and Jessica Gomez
Lead with Culture by Jay Billy
Lead with Instructional Rounds by Vicki Wilson
Lead with Literacy by Mandy Ellis
She Leads by Dr. Rachael George and Majalise W. Tolan

The EduProtocol Field Guide Series
Deploying EduProtocols by Kim Voge, with Jon Corippo and Marlena Hebern
The EduProtocol Field Guide by Marlena Hebern and Jon Corippo

The EduProtocol Field Guide Book 2 by Marlena Hebern and Jon Corippo
The EduProtocol Field Guide ELA Edition by Jacob Carr
The EduProtocol Field Guide Math Edition by Lisa Nowakowski and Jeremiah Ruesch
The EduProtocol Field Guide Primary Edition by Benjamin Cogswell and Jennifer Dean
The EduProtocol Field Guide Social Studies Edition by Dr. Scott M. Petri and Adam Moler

Leadership & School Culture

Be 1% Better by Ron Clark
Beyond the Surface of Restorative Practices by Marisol Rerucha
Change the Narrative by Henry J. Turner and Kathy Lopes
Choosing to See by Pamela Seda and Kyndall Brown
Culturize by Jimmy Casas
Discipline Win by Andy Jacks
Educate Me! by Dr. Shree Walker with Micheal D. Ison
Escaping the School Leader's Dunk Tank by Rebecca Coda and Rick Jetter
Fight Song by Kim Bearden
From Teacher to Leader by Starr Sackstein
If the Dance Floor Is Empty, Change the Song by Joe Clark
The Innovator's Mindset by George Couros
It's OK to Say "They" by Christy Whittlesey
Kids Deserve It! by Todd Nesloney and Adam Welcome
Leading the Whole Teacher by Allyson Apsey
Let Them Speak by Rebecca Coda and Rick Jetter
The Limitless School by Abe Hege and Adam Dovico
Live Your Excellence by Jimmy Casas
Next-Level Teaching by Jonathan Alsheimer
The Pepper Effect by Sean Gaillard
Principaled by Kate Barker, Kourtney Ferrua, and Rachael George
The Principled Principal by Jeffrey Zoul and Anthony McConnell
Relentless by Hamish Brewer
The Secret Solution by Todd Whitaker, Sam Miller, and Ryan Donlan
Start. Right. Now. by Todd Whitaker, Jeffrey Zoul, and Jimmy Casas
Stop. Right. Now. by Jimmy Casas and Jeffrey Zoul

Teach Your Class Off by CJ Reynolds
Teachers Deserve It by Rae Hughart and Adam Welcome
They Call Me "Mr. De" by Frank DeAngelis
Thrive through the Five by Jill M. Siler
Unmapped Potential by Julie Hasson and Missy Lennard
When Kids Lead by Todd Nesloney and Adam Dovico
Word Shift by Joy Kirr
Your School Rocks by Ryan McLane and Eric Lowe

Technology & Tools

50 Things to Go Further with Google Classroom by Alice Keeler and Libbi Miller
50 Things You Can Do with Google Classroom by Alice Keeler and Libbi Miller
50 Ways to Engage Students with Google Apps by Alice Keeler and Heather Lyon
140 Twitter Tips for Educators by Brad Currie, Billy Krakower, and Scott Rocco
Block Breaker by Brian Aspinall
Building Blocks for Tiny Techies by Jamila "Mia" Leonard
Code Breaker by Brian Aspinall
The Complete EdTech Coach by Katherine Goyette and Adam Juarez
Control Alt Achieve by Eric Curts
The Esports Education Playbook by Chris Aviles, Steve Isaacs, Christine Lion-Bailey, and Jesse Lubinsky
Google Apps for Littles by Christine Pinto and Alice Keeler
Master the Media by Julie Smith
Raising Digital Leaders by Jennifer Casa-Todd
Reality Bytes by Christine Lion-Bailey, Jesse Lubinsky, and Micah Shippee, PhD
Sail the 7 Cs with Microsoft Education by Becky Keene and Kathi Kersznowski
Shake Up Learning by Kasey Bell
Social LEADia by Jennifer Casa-Todd
Stepping Up to Google Classroom by Alice Keeler and Kimberly Mattina
Teaching Math with Google Apps by Alice Keeler and Diana Herrington
Teaching with Google Jamboard by Alice Keeler and Kimberly Mattina

Teachingland by Amanda Fox and Mary Ellen Weeks

Teaching Methods & Materials

All 4s and 5s by Andrew Sharos
Boredom Busters by Katie Powell
Building Strong Writers by Christina Schneider
The Classroom Chef by John Stevens and Matt Vaudrey
The Collaborative Classroom by Trevor Muir
Copyrighteous by Diana Gill
CREATE by Bethany J. Petty
Ditch That Homework by Matt Miller and Alice Keeler
Ditch That Textbook by Matt Miller
Don't Ditch That Tech by Matt Miller, Nate Ridgway, and Angelia Ridgway
EDrenaline Rush by John Meehan
Educated by Design by Michael Cohen, The Tech Rabbi
Empowered to Choose: A Practical Guide to Personalized Learning by Andrew Easton
Expedition Science by Becky Schnekser
Frustration Busters by Katie Powell
Fully Engaged by Michael Matera and John Meehan
Game On? Brain On! by Lindsay Portnoy, PhD
Guided Math AMPED by Reagan Tunstall
Happy & Resilient by Roni Habib
Innovating Play by Jessica LaBar-Twomy and Christine Pinto
Instant Relevance by Denis Sheeran
Instructional Coaching Connection by Nathan Lang-Raad
Keeping the Wonder by Jenna Copper, Ashley Bible, Abby Gross, and Staci Lamb
LAUNCH by John Spencer and A.J. Juliani
Learning in the Zone by Dr. Sonny Magana
Lights, Cameras, TEACH! by Kevin J. Butler
Make Learning MAGICAL by Tisha Richmond
Pass the Baton by Kathryn Finch and Theresa Hoover
Project-Based Learning Anywhere by Lori Elliott
Pure Genius by Don Wettrick
The Revolution by Darren Ellwein and Derek McCoy

The Science Box by Kim Adsit and Adam Peterson
Shift This! by Joy Kirr
Skyrocket Your Teacher Coaching by Michael Cary Sonbert
Spark Learning by Ramsey Musallam
Sparks in the Dark by Travis Crowder and Todd Nesloney
Table Talk Math by John Stevens
Teachables by Cheryl Abla and Lisa Maxfield
Unpack Your Impact by Naomi O'Brien and LaNesha Tabb
The Wild Card by Hope and Wade King
Writefully Empowered by Jacob Chastain
The Writing on the Classroom Wall by Steve Wyborney
You Are Poetry by Mike Johnston
You'll Never Guess What I'm Saying by Naomi O'Brien
You'll Never Guess What I'm Thinking About by Naomi O'Brien

Inspiration, Professional Growth & Personal Development
Be REAL by Tara Martin
Be the One for Kids by Ryan Sheehy
The Coach ADVenture by Amy Illingworth
Creatively Productive by Lisa Johnson
The Ed Branding Book by Dr. Renae Bryant and Lynette White
Educational Eye Exam by Alicia Ray
The EduNinja Mindset by Jennifer Burdis
Empower Our Girls by Lynmara Colón and Adam Welcome
Finding Lifelines by Andrew Grieve and Andrew Sharos
The Four O'Clock Faculty by Rich Czyz
How Much Water Do We Have? by Pete and Kris Nunweiler
P Is for Pirate by Dave and Shelley Burgess
A Passion for Kindness by Tamara Letter
The Path to Serendipity by Allyson Apsey
PheMOMenal Teacher by Annick Rauch
Recipes for Resilience by Robert A. Martinez
Rogue Leader by Rich Czyz
Sanctuaries by Dan Tricarico
Saving Sycamore by Molly B. Hudgens
The Secret Sauce by Rich Czyz

Shattering the Perfect Teacher Myth by Aaron Hogan
Stories from Webb by Todd Nesloney
Talk to Me by Kim Bearden
Teach Better by Chad Ostrowski, Tiffany Ott, Rae Hughart, and Jeff Gargas
Teach Me, Teacher by Jacob Chastain
Teach, Play, Learn! by Adam Peterson
The Teachers of Oz by Herbie Raad and Nathan Lang-Raad
Teaching the Ms. Abbott Way by Joyce Stephens Abbott
TeamMakers by Laura Robb and Evan Robb
Through the Lens of Serendipity by Allyson Apsey
Write Here and Now by Dan Tricarico
The Zen Teacher by Dan Tricarico

Children's Books

The Adventures of Little Mickey by Mickey Smith Jr.
Alpert by LaNesha Tabb
Alpert & Friends by LaNesha Tabb
Beyond Us by Aaron Polansky
Cannonball In by Tara Martin
Dolphins in Trees by Aaron Polansky
Dragon Smart by Tisha and Tommy Richmond
I Can Achieve Anything by MoNique Waters
I Want to Be a Lot by Ashley Savage
The Magic of Wonder by Jenna Copper, Ashley Bible, Abby Gross, and Staci Lamb
Micah's Big Question by Naomi O'Brien
The Princes of Serendip by Allyson Apsey
Ride with Emilio by Richard Nares
A Teacher's Top Secret Confidential by LaNesha Tabb
A Teacher's Top Secret: Mission Accomplished by LaNesha Tabb
The Wild Card Kids by Hope and Wade King
Zom-Be a Design Thinker by Amanda Fox

www.ingramcontent.com/pod-product-compliance
Lightning Source LLC
Chambersburg PA
CBHW050554160426
43199CB00015B/2653